Ju GERMAN

HOW TO GET BY AND
BE EASILY UNDERSTOOD

New York Chicago San Francisco Lisbon London Madrid Mexico City
Milan New Delhi San Juan Seoul Singapore Sydney Toronto

The McGraw·Hill Companies

Library of Congress Cataloging-in-Publication Data

Ellis, D. L.
    Just enough German / by D. L. Ellis, A. Cheyne. — 2nd ed.
        p.   cm.—(Just enough series)
    Includes bibliographical references and index.
    ISBN 0-07-149222-4 (alk. paper)
    1. German language—Conversation and phrase books—
English.
  I. Cheyne, A.   II. Title.

    PF3121.E65   2007
    438.3′421—dc22   2007001706

6 7 8 9 10 11   DOC/DOC   1 4 3 2 1 0

ISBN-13: 978-0-07-149222-5
ISBN-10:   0-07-149222-4

McGraw-Hill books are available at special quantity discounts to use
as premiums and sales promotions, or for use in corporate training
programs. For more information, please write to the Director of
Special Sales, Professional Publishing, McGraw-Hill, Two Penn Plaza,
New York, NY 10121-2298. Or contact your local bookstore.

This book is printed on acid-free paper.

Contents

Using This Phrase Book

Although primarily designed to help you get by in Germany—to get what you want or need—this phrase book is also useful in Austria and Switzerland. It concentrates on the simplest but most effective way you can express your needs in an unfamiliar language.

The Contents tells you which section to consult for the phrase you need. The Index gives more detailed information about where to look for your phrase.

When you have found the right page, you are given either the exact phrase or help in making a suitable sentence, as well as help with the pronunciation.

The German sentences in **bold type** will be useful in a variety of different situations, so they are worth learning by heart. See also the "Do It Yourself" section at the end of the book.

Especially note the sections "Everyday Expressions," "Shop Talk," and "Public Notices." You can expect to refer to them frequently.

When you are abroad, remember to make good use of the local tourist offices (see "The Tourist Information Office," p. 13). Before you leave, you can contact one of the following offices.

German National Tourist Office
122 E. 42nd Street
New York, NY
(212) 661-7200

Swiss National Tourist Office
608 Fifth Avenue
New York, NY 10020
(212) 757-5944

Austrian National Tourist Office
500 Fifth Avenue
New York, NY 10110
(212) 944-6880

A Note on the Pronunciation System

Many travelers' phrase books usually have a pronunciation section that tries to teach English-speaking tourists how to correctly pronounce the language of the country they are visiting. This is based on the belief that to be understood, the tourist must have an accurate, authentic accent, pronouncing every word perfectly.

The authors of this book, on the other hand, decided to devise a workable and usable pronunciation system. We had to face the fact that it is impossible for an average English speaker, who has no technical training in phonetics and phonetic transcription systems, to reproduce the sounds of a foreign language with perfect accuracy just from reading a phonetic transcription. We also believe that you don't have to have perfect pronunciation to make yourself understood in a foreign country. After all, the native speakers you meet will understand that you are a visitor; they will more likely appreciate your efforts to communicate and will go out of their way to try to understand you. They may even help you and correct you in a friendly manner. We have also found that visitors to a foreign country are not usually concerned about perfect pronunciation—they just want to get their message across—to communicate!

This is why we have designed a pronunciation system of the utmost simplicity. This system does not try to give an accurate—while also problematic and tedious—representation of German sounds; instead, it uses the common English sound and letter combinations that are the closest to the German sounds. Therefore, the German phrases transcribed for pronunciation should be read as naturally as possible, as if they were in ordinary English. In no way do you have to make the words sound "foreign." So while to yourself you sound as if you are speaking ordinary English—or at least making ordinary English sounds—you are also making yourself understood in German. Practice makes perfect: it is a good idea to repeat aloud to yourself several times the phrases you think you will use, before you actually use them. This will give you greater confidence and will help you make yourself understood.

In German, it is important to stress or emphasize the vowels in italics, just as you would in the English example, "Li*ttle* Jack H*or*ner s*a*t in the c*or*ner." Here are ten syllables, but only four stresses. Also, take note that the character **ß** is unique to German; it is pronounced like the English *ss*.

Of course, you may enjoy trying to pronounce German as well as possible, and the present system is a good way to start. Since it uses only English sounds, however, you will very soon need to depart from it as you imitate the sounds of German speakers and begin to relate them to the German spellings. German should pose no problems, as its pronunciation and spelling have an obvious and consistent relation.

Viel Spaß!

Everyday Expressions

• See also "Shop Talk," p. 41.

Hello./Good day./ Good afternoon.	**Guten Tag.** goo-ten tahk
Hello. (Austria)	**Grüß Gott.** grooss goht
Good morning.	**Guten Morgen.** goo-ten morgen
Good evening.	**Guten Abend.** goo-ten ah-bent
Good night.	**Gute Nacht.** goo-teh nahkt
Good-bye.	**Auf Wiedersehen.** owf veeder-zain **Tschüss.** choos
See you later.	**Bis später.** bis shpater
Yes.	**Ja.** yah
Please.	**Bitte.** bitteh
Yes, please.	**Ja, bitte.** yah bitteh
Great!	**Prima!** pree-mah
Thank you.	**Danke.** dunkeh
Thank you very much.	**Vielen Dank.** feelen dunk
That's right.	**Das stimmt.** dahs shtimmt
No.	**Nein.** nine
No, thank you.	**Nein, danke.** nine dunkeh
I disagree.	**Das stimmt nicht.** dahs shtimmt nisht
Excuse me./Sorry.	**Entschuldigen Sie.** ent-shool-dig-en zee
Don't mention it./That's OK.	**Bitte sehr.** bitteh zair

2 Everyday Expressions

That's good./I like it.	**Das gefällt mir.**
	dahs ga-fellt meer
That's no good./I don't like it.	**Das gefällt mir nicht.**
	dahs ga-fellt meer nisht
I know.	**Ich weiß.**
	ish vice
I don't know.	**Ich weiß nicht.**
	ish vice nisht
It doesn't matter.	**Es macht nichts.**
	es mahkt nishts
Where's the restroom, please?	**Wo sind die Toiletten?**
	vo zint dee twah-letten
How much is that? [point]	**Wie viel kostet das?**
	vee feel kohstet das
Is the service included?	**Ist die Bedienung inbegriffen?**
	ist dee be-dee-noong in-ba-griffen
Do you speak English?	**Sprechen Sie Englisch?**
	shpreshen zee eng-lish
I'm sorry . . .	**Es tut mir leid, . . .**
	es toot meer lite
. . . I don't speak German.	**ich spreche nicht Deutsch.**
	ish shpresheh nisht doytsh
. . . I only speak a little German.	**ich spreche nur ein wenig Deutsch.**
	ish shpresheh noor ine vay-nik doytsh
. . . I don't understand.	**ich verstehe nicht.**
	ish fair-shtay-heh nisht
Please can you . . .	**Bitte können Sie . . .**
	bitteh kernnen zee
. . . repeat that?	**das wiederholen?**
	dahs veeder-holen
. . . speak more slowly?	**langsamer sprechen?**
	lung-zahmer shpreshen
. . . write it down?	**das aufschreiben?**
	dahs owf-shry-ben
What is this called in German? [point]	**Wie heißt das auf Deutsch?**
	vee hysst dahs owf doytsh

Crossing the Border

Essential Information

- Don't waste time, just before you leave, rehearsing what you're going to say to the border officials—the chances are that you won't have to say anything at all, especially if you travel by air.
- It's more useful to check that you have your documents handy for the journey: passport, tickets, money, traveler's checks, insurance documents, driver's license, and car registration documents.
- Look out for the following signs.

Zoll	Customs
Grenze	Border
Grenzpolizei	Border police

For more signs and notices, see "Reference," p. 103.

- Customs officials may ask you routine questions, such as those that follow. If you have to give personal details, see "Meeting People," p. 5. Another important answer to know is "Nothing": **Nichts** (nishts).

Routine Questions

Passport?	**Pass?** pahss
Insurance card?	**Versicherungskarte?** fair-*zisher*-oongs-k*arteh*
Vehicle registration papers?	**Kraftfahrzeugschein?** k*rah*ft-far-tsoyk-shine
Have you anything to declare?	**Haben Sie etwas zu verzollen?** h*ah*ben zee *et*vahs tsoo fair-*tsolen*
Where are you going?	**Wohin fahren Sie?** v*o*-hin *far*-en zee
How long are you staying?	**Wie lange bleiben Sie?** vee *lung*-eh *bly*-ben zee
Where have you come from?	**Woher kommen Sie?** v*o*-hair *komen* zee

You also may have to fill in forms that ask for the following information.

surname	**(Familien-) Name**
first name	**Vorname**
maiden name	**Mädchenname**
place of birth	**Geburtsort**

date of birth	**Geburtsdatum**
address	**Adresse/Anschrift**
nationality	**Staatsangehörigkeit**
profession	**Beruf**
passport number	**Passnummer**
issued at	**ausgestellt in**
signature	**Unterschrift**

Meeting People

See also "Everyday Expressions," p. 1.

Breaking the Ice

Hello.	**Guten Tag. (Hallo.)** *goo*-ten t*ahk* (hullo)
Hello. (Austria)	**Grüß Gott.** grooss g*oht*
Good morning.	**Guten Morgen.** *goo*-ten morgen
How are you?	**Wie geht es Ihnen? (Wie geht's?)** vee g*ait* es *ee*nen (vee g*ai*ts)
Pleased to meet you.	**Angenehm.** *un*-ga-name
I am here . . .	**Ich bin hier ...** ish bin here
. . . on vacation.	**auf Urlaub.** owf *oor*-lowp
. . . on business.	**auf Geschäftsreise.** owf ga-shefts-ryzeh
Can I offer you . . .	**Kann ich Ihnen ... anbieten?** kahn ish *ee*nen ... *ahn*-beeten
. . . a drink?	**etwas zu trinken** *et*vahs tsoo tr*i*nken
. . . a cigarette?	**eine Zigarette** *i*neh tsee-g*a*retteh
. . . a cigar?	**eine Zigarre** *i*neh tsee-g*a*rreh
Are you staying long?	**Bleiben Sie hier lange?** bly-ben zee here l*u*ng-eh

Names

What's your name?	**Wie ist Ihr Name?** vee ist eer n*ah*meh
My name is . . .	**Mein Name ist ...** mine n*ah*meh ist

Family

Are you married?	**Sind Sie verheiratet?** zint zee fer-hy-rah-tet

I am . . .	**Ich bin ...** ish bin
. . . married.	**verheiratet.** fair-hy-rah-tet
. . . single.	**ledig.** laid-ik
This is . . .	**Dies ist ...** dees ist
. . . my wife.	**meine Frau.** mineh frow
. . . my husband.	**mein Mann.** mine munn
. . . my son.	**mein Sohn.** mine zone
. . . my daughter.	**meine Tochter.** mineh tokter
. . . my (boy) friend.	**mein Freund.** mine froynt
. . . my (girl) friend.	**meine Freundin.** mineh froyndin
. . . my (male) colleague.	**mein Kollege.** mine coal-laig-eh
. . . my (female) colleague.	**meine Kollegin.** mineh coal-laig-in
Do you have any children?	**Haben Sie Kinder?** hahben zee kin-der
I have . . .	**Ich habe ...** ish hahbeh
. . . one daughter.	**eine Tochter.** ineh tohkter
. . . one son.	**einen Sohn.** inen zone
No, I haven't any children.	**Nein, ich habe keine Kinder.** nine ish hahbeh kineh kin-der

Where You Live

Are you . . .	**Sind Sie ...** zind zee
. . . German?	**Deutscher/Deutsche?*** doyt-sher/doyt-sheh
. . . Swiss?	**Schweizer/Schweizerin?*** shvytser/shvytser-in

I am . . .	**Ich bin ...**
	ish bin
. . . American.	**Amerikaner/Amerikanerin.***
	ameri-*kah*-ner/ameri-*kah*-ner-in
. . . Canadian.	**Kanadier.**
	kah-*nah*-dee-er
. . . English.	**Engländer/Engländerin.***
	eng-lender/eng-lender-in
I'm . . .	**Ich bin ...**
	ish bin
. . . from Canada.	**aus Kanada.**
	ows *kah*-nah-dah
. . . from England.	**aus England.**
	ows eng-lunt
. . . from the United States.	**aus den Vereinigten Staaten.**
	ows dehn fair-*ine*-ik-ten sht*ah*-ten

For more, see "Countries and Nationalities," p. 116.

For the Businessman and Businesswoman

I'm from . . . (firm's name)	**Ich bin von ...**
	ish bin fon
I have an appointment with . . .	**Ich habe eine Verabredung mit ...**
	ish h*ah*beh *i*neh fair-*up*-ray-doong mit
May I speak to . . . ?	**Kann ich mit ... sprechen?**
	kahn ish mit ... shpr*e*shen
This is my card.	**Hier ist meine Karte.**
	here ist m*i*neh k*a*rte
I'm sorry I'm late.	**Es tut mir leid, ich habe mich verspätet.**
	es toot meer l*i*te ish h*ah*beh mish fair-shp*ay*-tet
Can I make another appointment?	**Kann ich eine neue Verabredung treffen?**
	kahn ish *i*neh n*oy*-eh fair-*up*-ray-doong tr*e*ffen
I'm staying at the (Crown) Hotel.	**Ich wohne im Hotel (Krone).**
	ish vone-eh im hotel (krone-eh)
I'm staying on (Park) Road.	**Ich wohne in der (Park)straße.**
	ish vone-eh in dair (park) shtr*ah*sseh

*For men use the first word; for women, the second.

Asking Directions

Essential Information

- Watch for the names of the following places on shops, maps, and notices.

What to Say

Excuse me, please.	**Entschuldigen Sie, bitte.** ent-shool-dig-en zee bitteh
How do I get . . .	**Wie komme ich …** vee komeh ish
. . . to Hamburg?	**nach Hamburg?** nahk hum-boork
. . . to the (Station) Road?	**zur (Bahnhof)straße?** tsoor (bahn-hohf)shtrahsseh
. . . to the hotel (Krone)?	**zum Hotel (Krone)?** tsoom hotel (krone-eh)
. . . to the airport?	**zum Flughafen?** tsoom flook-hahfen
. . . to the beach?	**zum Strand?** tsoom shtrunt
. . . to the bus station?	**zum Busbahnhof?** tsoom boos-bahn-hohf
. . . to the historic site?	**zur historischen Stätte?** tsoor histo-rish-en shtetteh
. . . to the market?	**zum Markt?** tsoom markt
. . . to the police station?	**zur Polizeiwache?** tsoor polee-tsy-vahkkeh
. . . to the port?	**zum Hafen?** tsoom hahfen
. . . to the post office?	**zum Postamt?** tsoom post-umt
. . . to the railway station?	**zum Bahnhof?** tsoom bahn-hohf
. . . to the sports stadium?	**zum Stadion?** tsoom shtah-dee-on
. . . to the tourist information office?	**zum Fremdenverkehrsbüro?** tsoom fremden-fairkairs-buro
. . . to the city center?	**zum Stadtzentrum?** tsoom shtaht-tsent-room
. . . to the town hall?	**zum Rathaus?** tsoom raht-house

Excuse me, please.	**Entschuldigen Sie, bitte.** _ent-shool-dig-en zee b_itteh
Is there . . . nearby?	**Gibt es ... in der Nähe?** _geept es ... in dair nay-eh_
. . . an art gallery . . .	**eine Kunstgalerie** _ineh koonst-galeree_
. . . a bakery . . .	**eine Bäckerei** _ineh becker-rye_
. . . a bank . . .	**eine Bank** _ineh bunk_
. . . a bar . . .	**eine Bar** _ineh bar_
. . . a botanical garden . . .	**einen botanischen Garten** _inen botah-nishen garten_
. . . a bus stop . . .	**eine Bushaltestelle** _ineh boos-hahlteh-shtelleh_
. . . a butcher shop . . .	**eine Metzgerei** _ineh mets-ga-rye_
. . . a café . . .	**ein Café** _ine kahffeh_
. . . a cake shop . . .	**eine Konditorei** _ineh kohn-dee-toh-rye_
. . . a campsite . . .	**einen Campingplatz** _inen cumping-plahts_
. . . a candy store . . .	**einen Süßwarenladen** _inen zoos-vahren-lahden_
. . . a church . . .	**eine Kirche** _ineh keer-sheh_
. . . a cinema . . .	**ein Kino** _ine kee-no_
. . . a currency exchange . . .	**eine Wechselstube** _ineh veksel-shtoobeh_
. . . a delicatessen . . .	**ein Feinkostgeschäft** _ine fine-kohst-ga-sheft_
. . . a dentist's office . . .	**einen Zahnarzt** _inen tsahn-artst_
. . . a disco . . .	**eine Diskothek** _ineh disco-take_
. . . a doctor's office . . .	**eine Arztpraxis** _ineh artst-prahk-sis_
. . . a drugstore . . .	**eine Apotheke** _ineh ah-po-take-eh_
. . . a dry cleaner . . .	**eine Reinigung** _ineh ry-nee-goong_

. . . a fish shop . . .	**ein Fischgeschäft**
	*i*ne fish-ga-sheft
. . . a fruit and vegetable shop . . .	**eine Gemüsehandlung**
	*i*neh ga-moozeh-hunt-loong
. . . a garage (for repairs) . . .	**eine Autowerkstatt**
	*i*neh owtoh-vairk-shtaht
. . . a gas station . . .	**eine Tankstelle**
	*i*neh tunk-shtelleh
. . . a grocery . . .	**ein Lebensmittelgeschäft**
	*i*ne laibens-mittel-ga-sheft
. . . a hairdresser's . . .	**einen Frisör**
	*i*nen free-zer
. . . a hardware shop . . .	**eine Eisenwarenhandlung**
	*i*neh izen-vahren-handloong
. . . a hospital . . .	**ein Krankenhaus**
	*i*ne krunken-house
. . . a hotel . . .	**ein Hotel**
	*i*ne hotel
. . . an ice-cream parlor . . .	**eine Eisdiele**
	*i*neh ice-deeleh
. . . a laundry . . .	**eine Wäscherei**
	*i*neh vesheh-rye
. . . a local health insurance office . . .	**eine Krankenkasse**
	*i*neh krunken-kahsseh
. . . a mailbox . . .	**einen Briefkasten**
	*i*nen breef-kahsten
. . . a museum . . .	**ein Museum**
	*i*ne moo-zay-oom
. . . a newsstand . . .	**einen Zeitungskiosk**
	*i*nen tsy-toongs-kyosk
. . . a nightclub . . .	**einen Nachtklub**
	*i*nen nahkt-kloop
. . . a park . . .	**einen Park**
	*i*nen park
. . . a parking lot . . .	**einen Parkplatz**
	*i*nen park-plahts
. . . a public telephone . . .	**eine Telefonzelle**
	*i*neh telephone-tselleh
. . . a public toilet . . .	**öffentliche Toiletten**
	erfent-lish-eh twah-letten
. . . a restaurant . . .	**ein Restaurant**
	*i*ne rest-o-rung
. . . a snack bar . . .	**einen Schnellimbiss**
	*i*nen shnell-im-bis

. . . a sports field . . .	**einen Sportplatz** *i*nen shp*o*rt-plahts
. . . a supermarket . . .	**einen Supermarkt** *i*nen z*oo*per-markt
. . . a swimming pool . . .	**ein Schwimmbad** ine shv*i*m-baht
. . . a taxi stand . . .	**einen Taxistand** *i*nen t*ah*xi-shtunt
. . . a theater . . .	**ein Theater** ine tay-*ah*ter
. . . a tobacco shop . . .	**einen Zigarettenladen** *i*nen tsee-gahretten-lahden
. . . a travel agency . . .	**ein Reisebüro** ine ryzeh-buro
. . . a youth hostel . . .	**eine Jugendherberge** *i*neh y*oo*gent-hair-bairgeh
. . . a zoo . . .	**einen Zoo** *i*nen ts*oh*

Directions

- Asking where a place is or if a place is nearby is one thing; making sense of the answer is another. Here are some of the most important key directions and replies you may get.

left	**links** links
right	**rechts** reshts
straight ahead	**geradeaus** grahdeh-*ows*
there	**dort** dort
first street left/right	**erste Straße links/rechts** *ai*rsteh shtr*ah*sseh l*i*nks/reshts
at the crossroads	**bei der Kreuzung** by dair kr*oy*-tsoong
at the traffic lights	**bei der Ampel** by dair *u*mpel
at the traffic circle	**beim Kreisverkehr** bime kr*i*ce-fair-kair
at the grade crossing	**beim Bahnübergang** bime b*ah*n-oober-gung

It's near/far.	**Es ist nah/weit.**
	es ist n*ah*/v*i*te
one kilometer	**ein Kilometer**
	*i*ne kilo-m*a*ter
two kilometers	**zwei Kilometer**
	tsvy kilo-m*a*ter
Five minutes . . .	**fünf Minuten ...**
	foonf min*oo*ten
. . . on foot.	**zu Fuß.**
	tsoo f*oo*ss
. . . by car.	**mit dem Auto.**
	mit dem *ow*to
Take . . .	**Nehmen Sie ...**
	n*ay*-men zee
. . . the bus.	**den Bus.**
	dehn b*oo*ss
. . . the train.	**den Zug.**
	dehn ts*oo*k
. . . the tram.	**die Straßenbahn.**
	dee shtr*ah*ssen-bahn
. . . the subway.	**die U-Bahn.**
	dee *oo*-bahn

See also "Public Transportation," p. 94.

The Tourist Information Office

Essential Information

- Most towns and holiday resorts in Germany, Switzerland, and Austria have a tourist information office; in smaller towns the local travel agency (**Reisebüro**) provides the same information and services.
- Look for these words on signs:

  Fremdenverkehrsbüro
  Verkehrsamt
  Informationsbüro

- If your main concern is to find and book accommodations, a **Zimmernachweis** (accommodation service) is the best place to go to.
- Tourist offices offer you free information in the form of printed leaflets, pamphlets, brochures, lists, and plans.
- On rare occasions, you may have to pay for some types of documents.
- For finding a tourist office, see "Asking Directions," p. 8.

What to Say

Please, have you got . . .	**Bitte, haben Sie …** *bitteh hahben zee*
. . . a map of the town?	**einen Stadtplan?** *inen shtaht-plahn*
. . . a list of events?	**einen Veranstaltungskalender?** *inen fair-un-shtahltoongs- kahlender*
. . . a list of hotels?	**ein Hotelverzeichnis?** *ine hotel-fair-tsy-shnis*
. . . a list of campsites?	**ein Campingplatzverzeichnis?** *ine cumping-plahts-fair-tsy-shnis*
. . . a list of restaurants?	**ein Restaurantverzeichnis?** *ine resto-rung-fair-tsy-shnis*
. . . a list of coach excursions?	**eine Liste mit Ausflugsfahrten?** *ineh listeh mit ows-flooks-farten*
. . . a brochure about the town?	**einen Prospekt von dieser Stadt?** *inen pro-spekt von deezer shtahtt*
. . . a brochure about the region?	**einen Prospekt von dieser Gegend?** *inen pro-spekt von deezer gay-ghent*

. . . a train schedule?	**einen Zugfahrplan?** *i*nen ts*ook*-far-plahn
. . . a bus schedule?	**einen Busfahrplan?** *i*nen b*oo*ss-far-plahn
In English, please.	**Auf Englisch, bitte.** *ow*f eng-lish b*i*tteh
How much do I owe you?	**Wie viel schulde ich Ihnen?** *vee* feel sh*oo*ldeh ish *ee*nen
Can you recommend . . .	**Können Sie ... empfehlen?** k*er*nen zee ... em-pf*ai*len
. . . a cheap hotel?	**ein billiges Hotel** ine b*i*llig-es hotel
. . . a cheap restaurant?	**ein billiges Restaurant** ine b*i*llig-es resto-r*u*ng

Can you make a booking
  for me?
	**Können Sie eine Reservierung für
	  mich machen?**
	k*er*nen zee *i*neh reser-v*ee*-roong
	  foor mish m*ah*khen

Likely Answers

- When the answer is "no," you should be able to tell by the person's facial expression, tone of voice, or gesture, but the following are some language clues.

No.	**Nein.** nine
I'm sorry.	**(Es) tut mir leid.** (es) toot meer l*i*te

I don't have a list of campsites.	**Ich habe kein
	  Campingplatzverzeichnis.**
	ish h*ah*beh kine c*u*mping-plahts-
	  fair-tsy-shnis

I haven't got any left.	**Ich habe keine mehr.** ish h*ah*beh k*i*neh mair
It's free.	**Es ist umsonst.** es ist oom-z*oh*nst

Accommodations

Hotel

Essential Information

- If you want hotel-type accommodations, look for signs with the following words in capital letters.

Hotel	
Hotel Garni	A room and breakfast, no other meals provided
Motel	
Pension	A boardinghouse
Gasthof	An inexpensive type of inn with a limited number of rooms
Zimmer Frei	Rooms for rent in private houses, bed-and-breakfast

- A list of hotels in the town or district usually can be obtained at the local tourist information office (see p. 13).

- Unlisted hotels are usually slightly cheaper and probably almost as good as listed hotels.

- Not all hotels and boardinghouses provide meals apart from breakfast; inquire about this on arrival at the reception desk.

- The cost is displayed in the room itself. So before you agree to stay, you can check it while you're having a look around.

- The displayed cost is for the room itself—per night and not per person. It usually includes service charges and taxes, but quite often does not include breakfast.

- Breakfast is continental style, with rolls, butter and jam, and boiled eggs; cheese and cold meats are usually available on request. Some larger hotels also offer a **Frühstücksbuffet** where you can help yourself to cereals, yogurt, fresh fruit, and so on.

- Upon arrival you will have to fill in an official registration form that bears an English translation. The receptionist will also want to see your passport.

- It is customary to tip the porter and leave a tip for the housekeeper in the hotel room.

- For asking directions to a hotel, see p. 8.

What to Say

I have a reservation.	**Ich habe reserviert.** ish h*ah*beh reserveert
Do you have any vacancies?	**Haben Sie noch Zimmer frei?** h*ah*ben zee nohk ts*i*mmer fry
Can I reserve a room?	**Kann ich ein Zimmer reservieren lassen?** kahn ish ine ts*i*mmer reser-v*ee*ren l*a*ssen
It's for . . .	**Es ist für ...** es ist foor
. . . one person.	**eine Person.** *i*neh per-z*o*ne
. . . two people.	**zwei Personen.** tsvy per-z*o*nen

For numbers, see p. 108.

It's for . . .	**Es ist für ...** es ist foor
. . . one night.	**eine Nacht.** *i*neh n*ah*kt
. . . two nights.	**zwei Nächte.** tsvy nesh-teh
. . . one week.	**eine Woche.** *i*neh v*o*ke-eh
. . . two weeks.	**zwei Wochen.** tsvy v*o*ken
I would like . . .	**Ich möchte ...** ish m*e*rshteh
. . . a room.	**ein Zimmer.** ine ts*i*mmer
. . . two rooms.	**zwei Zimmer.** tsvy ts*i*mmer
. . . a room with a single bed.	**ein Einzelzimmer.** ine *i*ne-tsel-ts*i*mmer
. . . a room with two single beds.	**ein Zweibettzimmer.** ine tsv*y*-bett-ts*i*mmer
. . . a room with a double bed.	**ein Doppelzimmer.** ine d*o*pel-ts*i*mmer
I would like a room . . .	**Ich möchte ein Zimmer ...** ish m*e*rshteh ine ts*i*mmer
. . . with a toilet.	**mit Toilette.** mit twah-l*e*tteh

. . . with a bathroom.	**mit Bad.** mit b*ah*t
. . . with a shower.	**mit Dusche.** mit d*oo*-sheh
. . . with a cot.	**mit einem Kinderbett.** mit *i*nem k*i*n-der-bett
. . . with a balcony.	**mit Balkon.** mit ball-k*o*ne
I would like . . .	**Ich möchte . . .** ish m*e*rshteh
. . . full board.	**Vollpension.** f*oa*l-penzee-*oh*n
. . . half board.	**Halbpension.** h*a*ll-penzee-*oh*n
. . . bed and breakfast.	**Übernachtung mit Frühstück.** oober-n*ah*ktoong mit fr*oo*shtook
Do you serve meals?	**Kann man bei Ihnen essen?** kahn mahn by *ee*nen essen
At what time is . . .	**Wann gibt es . . .** v*a*hnn geebt es
. . . breakfast?	**Frühstück?** fr*oo*-shtook
. . . lunch?	**Mittagessen?** m*i*ttahk-essen
. . . dinner?	**Abendessen?** *ah*bent-essen
How much is it?	**Wie viel kostet es?** v*ee* feel k*oh*stet es
Can I look at the room?	**Kann ich mir das Zimmer ansehen?** k*a*hn ish meer dahs ts*i*mmer un-zay-en
I'd prefer a room . . .	**Ich hätte lieber ein Zimmer . . .** ish hetteh l*ee*ber ine ts*i*mmer
. . . at the front/at the back.	**nach vorn/nach hinten.** nahk forn/nahk h*i*n-ten
OK, I'll take it.	**Gut, ich nehme es.** g*oo*t, ish n*ay*-meh es
No thanks, I won't take it.	**Nein danke, ich nehme es nicht.** n*i*ne d*u*nkeh ish n*ay*-meh es n*i*sht
The key to number (10), please.	**Den Schlüssel für Zimmer (Zehn), bitte.** dehn shl*oo*ssel foor ts*i*mmer (tsain) b*i*tteh

Please may I have . . .	**Kann ich bitte ... haben?**
	kahn ish bitteh ... hahben
. . . a coat hanger?	**einen Kleiderbügel**
	inen klyder-boogel
. . . a towel?	**ein Handtuch**
	ine hunt-took
. . . a glass?	**ein Glas**
	ine glahss
. . . some soap?	**ein Stück Seife**
	ine shtook zy-feh
. . . an ashtray?	**einen Aschenbecher**
	inen ahshen-besher
. . . another pillow?	**noch ein Kopfkissen**
	nohk ine kohpf-kissen
. . . another blanket?	**noch eine Decke**
	nohk ineh deckeh
Come in!	**Herein!**
	hair-rine
One moment, please!	**Einen Moment, bitte!**
	inen mo-ment bitteh
Please can you . . .	**Bitte, können Sie ...**
	bitteh kernnen zee
. . . do this laundry/dry cleaning?	**diese Sachen waschen lassen/ reinigen lassen?**
	deezeh zahkken vahshen lahssen/ ry-neeg-en lahssen
. . . call me at . . .?	**mich um ... anrufen**
	mish oom ... un-roofen
. . . help me with my luggage?	**mir mit meinem Gepäck behilflich sein?**
	meer mit minem ga-peck ba-hilf-lish zine
. . . call me a taxi for . . .?	**mir für ... ein Taxi bestellen?**
	meer foor ... ine tahxi ba-shtellen

For times, see p. 110.

The bill, please.	**Die Rechnung, bitte.**
	dee resh-noong bitteh
Is service included?	**Ist Bedienung inbegriffen?**
	ist ba-dee-noong in-begriffen
I think this is wrong.	**Ich glaube, hier ist ein Fehler.**
	ish glah-oobeh here ist ine failer
May I have a receipt?	**Kann ich eine Quittung haben?**
	kahn ish ineh kvit-oong hahben

At Breakfast

Some more . . . , please.	**Noch etwas … bitte.** nohk *etwahs* … *b*itteh
. . . coffee . . .	**Kaffee** k*ah*ffeh
. . . tea . . .	**Tee** tay
. . . bread . . .	**Brot** brote
. . . butter . . .	**Butter** b*oo*tter
. . . jam . . .	**Marmelade** marmeh-*lah*deh
May I have boiled eggs?	**Kann ich ein gekochtes Ei haben?** kahn ish ine ga-k*oh*kt-es *eye* h*ah*ben

Likely Reactions

Do you have identification?	**Haben Sie einen Pass oder Personalausweis?** hahben zee inen pass oder per- zonahl-ows-vice
What's your name?	**Wie ist Ihr Name?** vee ist eer n*ah*meh
Sorry, we're full.	**Es tut mir leid, wir sind ausgebucht.** es toot meer *l*ite veer zint *ows*- ga-bookt
I haven't any rooms left.	**Ich habe keine Zimmer mehr frei.** ish h*ah*beh k*i*neh tsimmer mair fry
Do you want to have a look?	**Wollen Sie es sich ansehen?** vollen zee es zish *un*-zay-en
How many people is it for?	**Für wie viele Personen soll es sein?** foor v*ee* feeleh perz*o*nen zohl es z*i*ne
From (seven o'clock) onward.	**Ab (sieben Uhr).** up (z*ee*ben *o*or)
From (midday) onward.	**Ab (zwölf Uhr mittags).** up (tsv*e*rlf oor m*i*t-tahks)
For times, see p. 110.	
It's (40) euros.	**Es kostet (vierzig) Euro.** es k*oh*stet (f*ee*r-tsik) *oy*-roh
For numbers, see p. 108.	

Camping and Youth Hosteling

Essential Information

Camping

- Look for the following signs.

  Campingplatz
  Zeltplatz

- Be prepared for the following charges.

  per person
  for the car (if applicable)
  for the tent or trailer plot
  for electricity
  for hot showers

- You must provide proof of identity, such as your passport.

- If you cannot find an official campsite and want to camp elsewhere, get the permission of the farmer, the landowner, or the local police first.

- Camping is forbidden in the rest areas off the freeways.

- Usually it is not possible to make advance reservations on campsites. Try and secure a site by mid-afternoon if you are traveling during the high season.

- Owners of campsites in Germany are not liable for losses. You should make your own insurance arrangements in advance.

Youth Hostels

- Look for the word **Jugendherberge**.

- You must have a Youth Hostel Association (YHA) card.

- Your YHA card must have your photograph; you can attach it yourself, if it does not require stamping.

- There is no upper age limit at German youth hostels, except in Bavaria where the age limit is twenty-seven.

- The charge for the night is the same regardless of the visitor's age, but some hostels are more expensive than others.

- Accommodation is usually in small dormitories.

- Many German youth hostels do not provide a kitchen in which visitors can prepare their own meals, but usually the houseparents provide meals at a reasonable price.
- You may have to help with domestic chores in some hostels.
- For replacing equipment, see p. 39.

What to Say

I have a reservation.	**Ich habe reserviert.** ish h*a*hbe reserveert
Have you any vacancies?	**Haben Sie noch etwas frei?** h*a*hben zee nohk *e*tvahs fry
It's for . . .	**Es ist für . . .** es ist foor
. . . one adult/one person.	**einen Erwachsenen/eine Person.** *i*nen er-v*a*hksen-en/*i*neh per-zone
. . . two adults/two people.	**zwei Erwachsene/zwei Personen.** tsvy er-v*a*hksen-eh/tsvy per-zonen
. . . and one child.	**und ein Kind.** oont ine kint
. . . and two children.	**und zwei Kinder.** oont tsvy k*i*n-der
. . . one night.	**eine Nacht.** *i*neh n*a*hkt
. . . two nights.	**zwei Nächte.** tsvy n*e*sh-teh
. . . one week.	**eine Woche.** *i*neh v*o*hk-eh
. . . two weeks.	**zwei Wochen.** tsvy v*o*hk-en
How much is it . . .	**Wie hoch ist die Gebühr . . .** vee hoke ist dee ga-boor
. . . for the tent?	**für das Zelt?** foor dahs tselt
. . . for the trailer?	**für den Wohnwagen?** foor dehn vone-v*a*hgen
. . . for the car?	**für das Auto?** foor dahs *o*wtoh
. . . for the electricity?	**für Elektrizität?** foor elektri-tsee-t*a*te
. . . per person?	**pro Person?** pro per-zone
. . . per day/night?	**pro Tag/Nacht?** pro t*a*hk/n*a*hkt

May I look around?	**Kann ich mich etwas umsehen?** kahn ish mish etvahs oom-zay-en
At what time do you lock up at night?	**Um wie viel Uhr schließen Sie nachts ab?** oom vee feel oor shleessen zee nahkts up
Do you provide anything . . .	**Kann man bei Ihnen etwas ... bekommen?** kahn mahn by eenen etvahs ... ba-komen
. . . to eat?	**zu essen** tsoo essen
. . . to drink?	**zu trinken** tsoo trinken
Do you have . . .	**Haben Sie ...** hahben zee
. . . a bar?	**eine Bar?** ineh bar
. . . hot showers?	**heiße Duschen?** hysseh doo-shen
. . . a kitchen?	**eine Küche?** ineh koo-sheh
. . . a laundry room?	**einen Waschsalon?** ineh vahsh-zahlone
. . . a restaurant?	**ein Restaurant?** ine resto-rung
. . . a shop?	**ein Geschäft?** ine ga-sheft
. . . a swimming pool?	**ein Schwimmbad?** ine shvimm-baht
. . . a snack bar?	**eine Imbissstube?** ineh im-bis-shtoobeh

See also "Shopping for Food," p. 45, and "Eating and Drinking Out," p. 62.

Where are . . .	**Wo sind ...** vo zint
. . . the wastebaskets?	**die Abfalleimer?** dee up-fall-imer
. . . the showers?	**die Duschen?** dee doo-shen
. . . the toilets?	**die Toiletten?** dee twah-letten

At what time must one . . .	**Um wie viel Uhr muss man ...** oom *vee* feel oor mooss mahn
. . . go to bed?	**schlafen gehen?** sh*lah*-fen gain
. . . get up?	**aufstehen?** *owf*-shtain
Please, have you got . . .	**Bitte haben Sie vielleicht ...** b*i*tteh h*ah*ben zee fee-*lysht*
. . . a broom?	**einen Besen?** *i*nen b*ay*-zen
. . . a can opener?	**einen Dosenöffner?** *i*nen d*o*ze-en-*erffner*
. . . a corkscrew?	**einen Korkenzieher?** *i*nen *korken*-tsee-er
. . . a dishcloth?	**ein Geschirrtuch?** ine ga-sh*eer*-took
. . . a fork?	**eine Gabel?** *i*neh g*ah*-bel
. . . a frying pan?	**eine Bratpfanne?** *i*neh br*a*ht-fun-eh
. . . an iron?	**ein Bügeleisen?** ine b*oo*gel-*i*zen
. . . a knife?	**ein Messer?** ine m*e*sser
. . . a plate?	**einen Teller?** *i*nen t*e*ller
. . . a refrigerator?	**einen Kühlschrank?** *i*nen k*oo*l-shrunk
. . . a saucepan?	**einen Kochtopf?** *i*nen k*oh*k-tohpf
. . . a teaspoon?	**einen Teelöffel?** *i*nen t*ay*-lerffel
. . . any dishwashing liquid?	**ein Spülmittel?** ine shp*oo*l-mittel
. . . any laundry detergent?	**Waschpulver?** v*ah*sh-poolver
The bill, please.	**Die Rechnung, bitte.** dee r*e*sh-noong b*i*tteh

Problems

The toilet . . .	**Die Toilette ...** dee twah-*l*etteh
The shower . . .	**Die Dusche ...** dee d*oo*-sheh

The faucet . . .	**Der Wasserhahn ...**
	dair *vahsser*-hahn
The electrical outlet . . .	**Die Steckdose ...**
	dee shteck-doze-eh
The light . . .	**Das Licht ...**
	dahs *lisht*
. . . is not working.	**... funktioniert nicht.**
	foonk-tsee-o-*neert* nisht
My camping gas has run out.	**Ich habe kein Camping-Gas mehr.**
	ish *hahbeh* kine *cumping*-gahs
	mair

Likely Reactions

Do you have identification?	**Haben Sie einen Pass oder**
	Personalausweis?
	hahben zee *inen* pahs *oder* per-
	zonahl-ows-vice
Your membership card, please.	**Ihre Mitgliedskarte, bitte.**
	eereh mit-gleets-karteh *bitteh*
What's your name?	**Wie ist Ihr Name?**
	vee ist eer *nahmeh*
Sorry, we're full.	**Es tut mir leid, wir sind voll**
	besetzt.
	es toot meer lite veer zint *foal*
	bezetst
How many people is it for?	**Für wie viele Personen?**
	foor *vee* feeleh per-*zonen*
How many nights is it for?	**Für wie viele Nächte?**
	foor *vee* feeleh *nesh*-teh
It's (4) euros . . .	**Es kostet (vier) Euro ...**
	es *kohstet* (feer) *oy*-roh
. . . per day/per night.	**pro Tag/pro Nacht.**
	pro *tahk*/pro *nahkt*

For numbers, see p. 108.

Rented Accommodations: Problem Solving
Essential Information

- If you're looking for lodging to rent, look for the following words on signs and advertisements.

Zu Vermieten	For rent
Appartemente	Apartments

| **Ferienwohnungen** | Vacation apartments |
| **Chalets** | |

- For arranging details of your rental, see "Hotel," p. 15.
- If you rent immediately, you will need to know the following words.

deposit	**die Kaution**
	dee kow-tsee-*on*
key	**der Schlüssel**
	dair shl*oo*sel

- Having arranged your own accommodations and arrived with the key, check the obvious basics that you take for granted at home.
- *Electricity:* Voltage? You may need an adapter for razors and small appliances brought from home.
- *Gas*: Municipal (natural) gas or bottled gas? Butane gas must be kept indoors, and propane gas must be kept outdoors.
- *Stove:* Don't be surprised to find the grill inside the oven or no grill at all, a lid covering the burners that lifts up to form a backsplash, or a mixture of two gas rings and two electric burners.
- *Toilet:* Main drainage or septic tank? Don't flush disposable diapers or anything else down the toilet if you have a septic tank.
- *Water:* Find the shutoff valve. Check faucets and plugs—they may not operate the way you are used to. Check how to turn on (or light) the hot water heater.
- *Windows:* Check how to open and close windows and shutters.
- *Insects:* Is an insecticide provided? If not, buy one.
- *Equipment:* For buying or replacing equipment, see p. 39.
- You will probably have an official agent, but find out whom to contact in an emergency; it may be a neighbor.

What to Say

My name is . . .	**Mein Name ist ...**
	mine n*ah*meh ist
I'm staying at . . .	**Ich wohne in ...**
	ish v*o*neh in
They've cut off . . .	**Man hat ... abgestellt.**
	mahn haht ... *u*p-ga-shtellt
. . . the electricity.	**den Strom**
	dehn shtr*o*me

. . . the gas.	**das Gas** dahs gahs
. . . the water.	**das Wasser** dahs vasser
Is there . . . in the area?	**Gibt es ... in der Nähe?** geept es ... in dair nay-eh
. . . an electrician . . .	**einen Elektriker** inen elek-trik-er
. . . a plumber . . .	**einen Klempner** inen klemp-ner
. . . a gas service technician . . .	**einen Installateur** inen in-stallah-ter
Where is . . .	**Wo ist ...** vo ist
. . . the fuse box?	**der Sicherungskasten?** dair zisher-oongs-kahsten
. . . the shutoff valve?	**der Abstellhahn?** dair up-shtell-hahn
. . . the boiler?	**der Boiler?** dair boy-ler
. . . the water heater?	**der Warmwasserbereiter?** dair vahm-vahsser-ba-ryter
Is there . . .	**Gibt es hier ...** geebt es here
. . . municipal (natural) gas?	**Stadtgas?** shtaht-gahs
. . . bottled gas?	**Flaschengas?** flahshen-gahs
. . . a septic tank?	**eine Sickergrube?** ineh zicker-groobeh
. . . central heating?	**Zentralheizung?** tsentrahl-hy-tsoong
The stove . . .	**Der Herd ...** dair hairt
The hair dryer . . .	**Der Haartrockner ...** dair har-troke-ner
The heating . . .	**Die Heizung ...** dee hy-tsoong
The boiler . . .	**Der Boiler ...** dair boy-ler
The iron . . .	**Das Bügeleisen ...** dahs boogel-izen
The pilot light . . .	**Die Zündflamme ...** dee tsoont-flahmmeh

The refrigerator . . .	**der Kühlschrank ...** dair kool-shrunk
The telephone . . .	**Das Telefon ...** dahs telephone
The toilet . . .	**Die Toilette ...** dee twah-letteh
The washing machine . . .	**Die Waschmaschine ...** dee vahsh-machine-eh
The water heater . . .	**Der Warmwasserbereiter ...** dair vahm-vahsser-ba-ryter
. . . is not working.	**... funktioniert nicht.** foonk-tsee-o-neert nisht
Where can I get . . .	**Wo kann ich ... bekommen?** vo kahn ish ... ba-komen
. . . an adapter for this?	**hierfür einen Zwischenstecker** here-foor inen tsvishen-shtecker
. . . a bottle of butane gas?	**eine Flasche Butangas** ineh flahsheh bootahn-gahs
. . . a bottle of propane gas?	**eine Flasche Propangas** ineh flahsheh pro-pahn-gahs
. . . a fuse?	**eine Sicherung** ineh zisher-oong
. . . an insecticide spray?	**ein Insektenspray** ine in-zekten-shpray
. . . a lightbulb?	**eine Glühbirne** ineh gloo-beerneh
The drain . . .	**Der Abfluss ...** dair up-flooss
The sink . . .	**Der Ausguss ...** der ows-gooss
The toilet . . .	**Die Toilette ...** dee twah-letteh
. . . is blocked.	**... ist verstopft.** ist fer-shtohpft
The gas is leaking.	**Die Gasleitung ist undicht.** dee gahs-lite-oong ist oon-disht
Can you fix it right away?	**Können Sie es sofort reparieren?** kernen zee es zofort repareeren
When can you fix it?	**Wann können Sie es reparieren?** vahnn kernen zee es repareeren
How much do I owe you?	**Wie viel schulde ich Ihnen?** vee feel shooldeh ish eenen
When is the garbage collected?	**Wann kommt die Müllabfuhr?** vahnn kohmt dee mool-up-foor

Likely Reactions

What's your name?	**Wie ist Ihr Name?** vee ist eer *nah*meh
What's your address?	**Wie ist Ihre Adresse?** vee ist *ee*reh uh*dress*eh
There's a shop . . .	**Es gibt einen Laden ...** es geebt *i*nen *lah*den
. . . in town.	**in der Stadt.** in dair sht*ah*t
. . . in the village.	**im Dorf.** im dorf
I can't come . . .	**Ich kann ... nicht kommen.** ish kahn ... nisht k*o*men
. . . today.	**heute** hoy-teh
. . . this week.	**diese Woche** d*ee*zeh v*o*ke-eh
I can't come until Monday.	**Ich kann erst Montag kommen.** ish kahn airst mone-tahk k*o*men
I can come . . .	**Ich kann ... kommen.** ish kahn ... k*o*men
. . . on Tuesday.	**Dienstag** d*ee*ns-tahk
. . . when you want.	**jederzeit** y*ai*der-tsyt
. . . every day.	**jeden Tag** y*ai*den tahk
. . . every other day.	**jeden zweiten Tag** y*ai*den tsvy-ten tahk
. . . on Wednesdays.	**mittwochs** m*i*tt-vokes

For the days of the week, see p. 112.

General Shopping

The Drugstore

Essential Information

- Look for the word **Apotheke** (drugstore, pharmacy) or this sign:

- There are two kinds of drugstores in Germany. The **Apotheke** is the place to go for prescriptions, medicines, and so on; toiletries and household items, as well as patent medicines, are sold at the **Drogerie**.

- Try the **Apotheke** *before* going to a doctor; pharmacists are usually qualified to treat minor injuries.

- Drugstores are open during normal business hours: from 8:30 a.m. to 12:30 p.m. and from 2:30 p.m. to 6:30 p.m. weekdays. On Saturdays, they close at 2:00 p.m.

- Drugstores take turns staying open all night and on Sundays. If a drugstore is closed, a notice on the door will give the address of the nearest drugstore with night (**Nachtdienst**) or Sunday service (**Sonntagsdienst**).

- Some toiletries can also be bought at a **Parfümerie**, but they will be more expensive.

- For finding a drugstore, see "Asking Directions," p. 8.

What to Say

I'd like . . .	**Ich möchte ...** ish m*e*rshteh
. . . some antacid.	**Antazidum.** ahnta-ts*ee*-doom
. . . some antiseptic.	**ein antiseptisches Mittel.** ine ahntee-ze*p*tishes m*i*ttel
. . . some aspirin.	**Aspirin.** ahs-pee-r*ee*n
. . . some bandages.	**Verbandstoff.** fair-b*ah*nts-shtohff
. . . some cotton balls.	**Wattebäusche.** v*ah*tteh b*oy*-sheh

. . . some eyedrops.	**Augentropfen.** *owghen-trohpfen*
. . . some foot powder.	**Fußpuder.** *fooss-pooder*
. . . some gauze.	**Verbandmull.** *fair-bahnt-mool*
. . . some inhalant.	**ein Inhaliermittel.** *ine in-hahleer-mittel*
. . . some insect repellent.	**ein Insektenschutzmittel.** *ine in-zekten-shoots-mittel*
. . . some lip balm.	**eine Lippensalbe.** *ineh lippen-zahlbeh*
. . . some nose drops.	**Nasentropfen.** *nahzen-trohpfen*
. . . some throat lozenges.	**Halspastillen.** *hahls-pahst-ill-en*
. . . some Vaseline.	**Vaseline.** *vahzeh-leeneh*
I'd like something for . . .	**Ich möchte etwas gegen …** *ish mershte etvahs gay-ghen*
. . . bites (snakes, dogs).	**Bisswunden.** *biss-voon-den*
. . . burns.	**Verbrennungen.** *fair-bren-oong-en*
. . . a cold.	**Erkältung.** *er-kelt-oong*
. . . constipation.	**Verstopfung.** *fair-shtohpf-oong*
. . . a cough.	**Husten.** *hoosten*
. . . diarrhea.	**Durchfall.** *doorsh-fahl*
. . . an earache.	**Ohrenschmerzen.** *or-en-shmairts-en*
. . . flu.	**Grippe.** *grippeh*
. . . scalds.	**Verbrühungen.** *fair-broo-oong-en*
. . . sore gums.	**wundes Zahnfleisch.** *voondes tsahn-flysh*
. . . sprains.	**Gelenkverstauchung.** *ga-lenk-fair-shtow-koong*
. . . stings (mosquitoes, bees).	**Insektenstiche.** *in-zekten-shtee-sheh*

. . . sunburn.	**Sonnenbrand.** zonen-brahnt
. . . travel/seasickness.	**Reisekrankheit/Seekrankheit.** ryzeh-krunk-hite/zeh-krunk-hite
I need . . .	**Ich brauche …** ish brow-keh
. . . some baby food.	**Babynahrung.** baby-nah-roong
. . . some contraceptives.	**ein Verhütungsmittel.** ine fair-hootoongs-mittel
. . . some deodorant.	**einen Deodorant.** inen deo-doh-runt
. . . some disposable diapers.	**Papierwindeln.** pahpeer-vin-deln
. . . some hand cream.	**eine Handkreme.** ineh hunt-craym
. . . some lipstick.	**einen Lippenstift.** inen lippen-shtift
. . . some makeup remover.	**eine Reinigungsmilch.** ineh ry-nee-goongs-milsh
. . . some razor blades.	**Rasierklingen.** rahzeer-kling-en
. . . some safety pins.	**Sicherheitsnadeln.** zisher-hyts-nahdeln
. . . some sanitary napkins.	**Monatsbinden.** mohnahts-bin-den
. . . some shaving cream.	**eine Rasierkreme.** ineh rahzeer-craym
. . . some soap.	**ein Stück Seife.** ine shtook zy-feh
. . . some sunscreen/suntan oil.	**Sonnenmilch/öl.** zonen-milsh/erl
. . . some talcum powder.	**Talkumpuder.** tahl-koom-pooder
. . . some tampons.	**eine Packung Tampons.** ineh pahck-oong tahm-pohnz
. . . some tissues.	**Papiertücher.** pahpeer-toosher
. . . some toilet paper.	**Toilettenpapier.** twah-letten-pahpeer
. . . some toothpaste.	**eine Tube Zahnpasta.** ineh toobeh tsahn-pasta

For other essential expressions, see "Shop Talk," p. 41.

Vacation Items

Essential Information

- The following are places to shop at and signs to look for.

Schreibwarengeschäft	Stationery
Photogeschäft	Films
Kunstgewerbe	Arts and crafts
Geschenkartikel	Gifts

- The following are the main department stores.

Karstadt
Horten
Hertie
Kaufhof

What to Say

Where can I buy . . . ?	**Wo kann ich ... kaufen?** vo kahn ish ... kow-fen
I'd like . . .	**Ich möchte ...** ish mershteh
. . . a bag.	**eine Tasche.** ineh tahsheh
. . . a beach ball.	**einen Strandball.** inen shtrunt-bahl
. . . a bucket.	**einen Eimer.** inen imer
. . . some envelopes.	**Briefumschläge.** breef-oom-shlaig-eh
. . . a guidebook.	**einen Reiseführer.** inen ryzeh-foorer
. . . a map (of the area).	**eine Landkarte von dieser Gegend.** ineh lunt-karteh fohn deezer gay-ghent
. . . a newspaper in English.	**eine Zeitung in englischer Sprache.** ineh tsy-toong in eng-lish-er shprahsh-eh
. . . some postcards.	**Ansichtskarten.** un-zishts-karten
. . . a shovel.	**eine Schaufel.** ineh sha-oofel
. . . a straw hat.	**einen Strohhut.** inen shtroh-hoot

. . . a suitcase.	**einen Koffer.**
	*i*nen k*o*fer
. . . some sunglasses.	**eine Sonnenbrille.**
	*i*neh zonen-brilleh
. . . a sunshade.	**einen Sonnenschirm.**
	*i*nen zonen-sheerm
. . . an umbrella.	**einen Regenschirm.**
	*i*nen r*ay*-ghen-sheerm
. . . some writing paper.	**Schreibpapier.**
	schr*i*pe-pahpeer
I'd like . . . [show your camera]	**Ich möchte …**
	ish m*e*rshteh
. . . color film.	**einen Farbfilm.**
	*i*nen farp-film
. . . black and white film.	**einen Schwarzweißfilm.**
	*i*nen shvarts-vice-film
. . . 12 (24/36) exposures.	**zwölf (vierundzwanzig/**
	sechsunddreißig) Aufnahmen.
	tsv*e*rlf (feer-oont-tsvun-sik/
	zex-oont-dry-sik) *o*wf-nahmen
. . . a memory card.	**eine Speicherkarte.**
	*i*neh shp*y*sher k*a*r-teh
. . . a videocassette.	**eine Videokassette.**
	*i*neh vih-day-o-kah-s*e*tteh
This camera is broken.	**Diese Kamera ist kaputt.**
	d*ee*zeh k*ah*mera ist kah-p*oo*t
The film is stuck.	**Der Film klemmt.**
	dair film klemmt
Please can you . . .	**Können Sie bitte …**
	k*e*rnen zee b*i*tteh
. . . develop/print this?	**diesen Film entwickeln/abziehen?**
	d*ee*zen film ent-v*i*ckeln/*u*p-tseen
. . . load the camera?	**den Film einlegen?**
	dehn film *i*ne-laygen

For other essential expressions, see "Shop Talk," p. 41.

The Tobacco Shop

Essential Information

- A tobacco shop is called a **Tabakwaren** or **Zigarrenladen**.
- Large supermarkets and department stores often have their own tobacco shops on the premises, a kind of stall near the entrance or cash registers.

- The tobacco shop is the only place where you can get tobacco, cigars, pipe utensils, flints, and so on, whereas cigarettes can be bought at a variety of places: at the **Kiosk**; at most food stores; from the cigarette machine round the corner; inside a café, bar, or pub, and so on.

- To ask if there is a tobacco shop nearby, see "Asking Directions," p. 8.

What to Say

A packet of cigarettes . . .	**Eine Schachtel Zigaretten ...**
	*i*neh sh*a*hktel tsee-gar-etten
. . . with filters.	**mit Filter.**
	mit f*i*lter
. . . without filters.	**ohne Filter.**
	o-neh f*i*lter
. . . king size.	**extra lang.**
	*e*xtra l*u*ng
. . . menthol.	**mit Menthol.**
	mit men-t*o*le
Those up there . . .	**Die da oben ...**
	dee dah *o*-ben
. . . on the right.	**rechts.**
	reshts
. . . on the left.	**links.**
	links
These. [*point*]	**Diese hier.**
	d*ee*zeh here
Cigarettes, please.	**Zigaretten, bitte.**
	tsee-garetten b*i*tteh
100, 200, 300	**einhundert, zweihundert, dreihundert**
	*i*ne-hoondert tsvy-hoondert dry-hoondert
Two packets.	**Zwei Schachteln.**
	tsvy sh*a*hkteln
Have you got . . .	**Haben Sie ...**
	h*a*hben zee
. . . English cigarettes?	**englische Zigaretten?**
	*e*ng-lisheh tsee-garetten
. . . American cigarettes?	**amerikanische Zigaretten?**
	ameri-k*a*h-nishen tsee-garetten
. . . rolling tobacco?	**Zigarettentabak?**
	tsee-garetten-tahbahk

The one down there . . .	**Den da unten ...** dehn dah *oo*nten
. . . on the right.	**rechts.** reshts
. . . on the left.	**links.** links
This one. [*point*]	**Diesen hier.** d*ee*zen here
A cigar, please.	**Eine Zigarre, bitte.** *i*neh tsee-g*a*rreh b*i*tteh
That one. [*point*]	**Die da.** d*ee* dah
Some cigars, please.	**Zigarren, bitte.** tsee-g*a*rren b*i*tteh
Those. [*point*]	**Die da.** d*ee* dah
A box of matches.	**Eine Schachtel Streichhölzer.** *i*neh sh*a*hktel shtrysh-h*er*ltser
A lighter.	**Ein Feuerzeug.** ine f*oy*-er-tsoyk

For other essential expressions, see "Shop Talk," p. 41.

Buying Clothes

Essential Information

• Look for the following words.

Damenbekleidung	Women's clothes
Herrenbekleidung	Men's clothes
Schuhgeschäft	Shoe shop

• Don't buy without being measured first or without trying things on.

• Don't rely on conversion charts of clothing sizes (see p. 123).

• If you are buying for other people, take their measurements with you.

• All major department stores sell clothes and shoes.

What to Say

I'd like . . .	**Ich möchte ...** ish m*e*rshteh
. . . an anorak.	**einen Anorak.** *i*nen *ah*-norahk

. . . a belt.	**einen Gürtel.**
	*in*en g*oo*r-tel
. . . a bikini.	**einen Bikini.**
	*in*en bik*i*ni
. . . a bra.	**einen Büstenhalter/BH.**
	*in*en b*oo*sten-halter/beh-h*ah*
. . . a cap (swimming).	**eine Badekappe.**
	*in*eh b*ah*deh-kahppeh
. . . a cap (skiing).	**eine Skimütze.**
	*in*eh sh*ee*-mootseh
. . . a cardigan.	**eine Wolljacke.**
	*in*eh v*oh*l-yahkeh
. . . a coat.	**einen Mantel.**
	*in*en m*u*ntel
. . . a dress.	**ein Kleid.**
	ine kl*i*te
. . . a hat.	**einen Hut.**
	*in*en hoot
. . . a jacket.	**eine Jacke.**
	*in*eh y*ah*-keh
. . . some pajamas.	**einen Schlafanzug.**
	*in*en shl*ah*f-un-tsook
. . . a raincoat.	**einen Regenmantel.**
	*in*en r*ay*-ghen-mahntel
. . . a shirt (women).	**eine Bluse.**
	*in*eh bl*oo*zeh
. . . a shirt (men).	**ein Oberhemd.**
	ine *o*-ber-hemt
. . . a skirt.	**einen Rock.**
	*in*en rohk
. . . a (woman's) suit.	**ein Kostüm.**
	ine kohst-*oo*m
. . . a (man's) suit.	**einen Anzug.**
	*in*en *u*n-tsook
. . . a sweater.	**einen Pullover.**
	*in*en pull-*o*ver
. . . a swimsuit.	**einen Badeanzug.**
	*in*en b*ah*deh-un-tsook
. . . some tights.	**eine Strumpfhose.**
	*in*eh shtr*oo*mpf-hozeh
. . . some trousers.	**eine Hose.**
	*in*eh hozeh
. . . a T-shirt.	**ein T-Shirt.**
	ine t*ee*-shirt

I'd like a pair of . . .	**Ich möchte ein Paar …** ish mershteh ine par
. . . (women's) briefs.	**Damenschlüpfer.** dahmen-shloopfer
. . . (men's) briefs.	**Herrenunterhosen.** hairen-oonter-hozen
. . . gloves.	**Handschuhe.** hunt-shoo-eh
. . . jeans.	**Jeans.** jeans
. . . shorts.	**Shorts.** shorts
. . . (short/long) socks.	**(kurze/lange) Socken.** koor-tseh/lungeh) zoken
. . . stockings.	**Strümpfe.** shtroom-feh
. . . shoes.	**Schuhe.** shoo-eh
. . . boots.	**Stiefel.** shtee-fel
. . . beach shoes.	**Strandsandalen.** shtrunt-zahndahlen
. . . dress shoes.	**elegante Schuhe.** ele-gahnteh shoo-eh
. . . moccasins.	**Mokassins.** mohkahssins
. . . sandals.	**Sandalen.** zahndahlen
. . . tennis shoes.	**Tennisschuhe.** tennis-shoo-eh
My size is . . .	**Ich habe Größe …** ish hahbeh grersseh
For numbers, see p. 108.	
Can you measure me, please?	**Können Sie bitte meine Maße nehmen?** kernen zee bitteh mineh mahsseh nay-men
Can I try it on?	**Kann ich es anprobieren?** kahn ish es un-pro-beeren
These are the measurements . . . [*show written measurements*] bust	**Hier sind die Maße …** here zint dee mahsseh **Oberweite** o-ber-vy-teh

chest	**Brustumfang**
	broost-oom-fung
collar	**Kragenweite**
	krah-ghen-vy-teh
hip	**Hüftumfang**
	hooft-oom-fung
leg	**Beinlänge**
	bine-leng-eh
waist	**Taillenweite**
	tahl-yen-vy-teh
Do you have something . . .	**Haben Sie etwas ...**
	hahben zee etvahs
. . . in black?	**in schwarz?**
	in shvarts
. . . in blue?	**in blau?**
	in bla-ow
. . . in brown?	**in braun?**
	in brown
. . . in gray?	**in grau?**
	in gra-oo
. . . in green?	**in grün?**
	in groon
. . . in pink?	**in rosa?**
	in roza
. . . in red?	**in rot?**
	in rote
. . . in white?	**in weiß?**
	in vice
. . . in yellow?	**in gelb?**
	in ghelp
. . . in this color? [point]	**in dieser Farbe?**
	in deezer farbeh
. . . in cotton?	**in Baumwolle?**
	in bowm-vohleh
. . . in denim?	**in Jeansstoff?**
	in jeans-shtohf
. . . in leather?	**in Leder?**
	in lay-der
. . . in nylon?	**in Nylon?**
	in nylon
. . . in suede?	**in Wildleder?**
	in vilt-lay-der
. . . in wool?	**in Wolle?**
	in vohleh

| . . . in this material? [point] | **in diesem Material?** |
| | in d*ee*zem mah-tairee-*ahl* |

For other essential expressions, see "Shop Talk," p. 41.

Replacing Equipment

Essential Information

- Look for the following shops and signs.

Eisenwarenhandlung	Hardware
Haushaltswaren	Household goods
Elektrogeschäft	Electrical items
Drogerie	Household cleaning supplies

- In a supermarket, look for this display: **Haushaltsartikel.**

- To ask the way to the shop, see "Asking Directions," p. 8.

- At a campsite, try its shop first.

What to Say

Have you got . . .	**Haben Sie ...**
	h*ah*ben zee
. . . an adapter? [show appliance]	**einen Zwischenstecker?**
	*i*nen tsv*i*shen-shtecker
. . . a bottle of butane gas?	**eine Flasche Butangas?**
	*i*neh fl*ah*sheh boot*ah*n-gahs
. . . a bottle of propane gas?	**eine Flasche Propangas?**
	*i*neh fl*ah*sheh pro-p*ah*n-gahs
. . . a bottle opener?	**einen Flaschenöffner?**
	*i*nen fl*ah*shen-*e*rffner
. . . a can opener?	**einen Dosenöffner?**
	*i*nen doze-en-*e*rffner
. . . a clothesline?	**eine Wäscheleine?**
	*i*neh vesheh-line-eh
. . . a corkscrew?	**einen Korkenzieher?**
	*i*nen korken-tsee-er
. . . a dish brush?	**eine Spülbürste?**
	*i*neh shp*oo*l-boorsteh
. . . any dish soap?	**ein Spülmittel?**
	ine shp*oo*l-mittel
. . . a dish towel?	**ein Geschirrtuch?**
	ine ga-sheer-took
. . . any disinfectant?	**ein Desinfektionsmittel?**
	ine des-infek-tsee-*oh*ns-mittel

. . . any disposable cups?	**Pappbecher?** *pahp*-besher
. . . any disposable plates?	**Pappteller?** *pahp*-teller
. . . a flashlight?	**eine Taschenlampe?** *ineh tahshen-lahmpeh*
. . . any flashlight batteries?	**Taschenlampenbatterien?** *tahshen-lahmpen-bahtter-ee-en*
. . . any forks?	**Gabeln?** *gah-beln*
. . . a fuse? [*show old fuse*]	**eine Sicherung?** *ineh zisher-oong*
. . . any insecticide spray?	**ein Insektenspray?** *ine in-zekten-shpray*
. . . any knives?	**Messer?** *messer*
. . . any laundry detergent?	**Waschpulver?** *vahsh-poolver*
. . . a lightbulb? [*show old one*]	**eine Glühbirne?** *ineh gloo-beer-neh*
. . . any paper towels?	**eine Rolle Küchenpapier?** *ineh rolleh koo-shen-pahpeer*
. . . a plastic bucket?	**einen Plastikeimer?** *inen plahstik-imer*
. . . a plastic can?	**einen Plastikkanister?** *inen plahstik-kahnister*
. . . a plug (for the sink)?	**einen Stöpsel (für das Spülbecken)?** *inen shterp-zel foor dahs shpool-becken*
. . . a scouring pad?	**einen Scheuerschwamm?** *inen shoy-er-shrahm*
. . . a sponge?	**einen Schwamm?** *inen shvahmm*
. . . any string?	**Bindfaden?** *bint-fahden*
. . . any tent pegs?	**Heringe fürs Zelt?** *hairing-eh foors tselt*
. . . a wrench?	**einen Schraubenschlüssel?** *inen shrowben-shloosel*

For other essential expressions, see "Shop Talk," p. 41.

Shop Talk

Essential Information

- Know your coins and bills. Germany uses the euro. Switzerland, however, retains its own currency.

EU coins	1, 2, 5, 10, 20, 50 cents; 1, 2 euros
EU bills	5, 10, 20, 50, 100, 200, 500 euros
Swiss coins	5, 10, 20, 50 rappen; 1, 2, 5 franken
Swiss bills	10, 20, 50, 100, 500, 1,000 franken

- The coins of the European Union have a common side that gives the denomination. The flip side of the coin is the country-specific side that contains images particular to a member nation.

- Know how to say the important weights and measures. Note that though Germany uses the metric system, people still use the word **Pfund** (pound).

- Important weights and measures are as follows.

50 grams	**fünfzig Gramm** *foonf-tsik gr*a*hm*
100 grams	**einhundert Gramm** *ine-hoondert gr*a*hm*
200 grams	**zweihundert Gramm** *tsvy-hoondert gr*a*hm*
½ pound (250 grams)	**ein halbes Pfund** *ine h*a*llbes pfoont*
1 pound	**ein Pfund** *ine pfoont*
1 kilo	**ein Kilo** *ine k*i*lo*
2 kilos	**zwei Kilo** *tsvy k*i*lo*
½ liter	**einen halben Liter** *inen h*a*llben l*i*ter*
1 liter	**einen Liter** *inen l*i*ter*
2 liters	**zwei Liter** *tsvy l*i*ter*

For numbers, see p. 108.

- In small shops, don't be surprised if customers as well as the shop assistants say "hello" and "good-bye" to you.

What to Say

Customer

Hello.	**Guten Tag.** *goo-*ten t*ahk*
Hello. (Austria)	**Grüß Gott.** *grooss* goht
Good morning.	**Guten Morgen.** *goo-*ten morgen
Good afternoon.	**Guten Tag.** *goo-*ten t*ahk*
Good-bye.	**Auf Wiedersehen.** owf veeder-zain
I'm just looking.	**Ich sehe mich nur um.** ish zay-eh mish noor oom
Excuse me.	**Entschuldigen Sie.** ent-shool-dig-en zee
How much is this/that?	**Wie viel kostet dies/das?** vee feel kohstet dees/dahs
What is that?/What are those?	**Was ist das?** vahs ist dahs
Is there a discount?	**Gibt es einen Rabatt?** geept es inen rah-baht
I'd like that, please.	**Ich möchte das da, bitte.** ish mershteh dahs dah bitteh
Not that.	**Nicht das.** nisht dahs
Like that.	**Wie das da.** vee dahs dah
That's enough, thank you.	**Das ist genug, danke.** dahs ist ga-nook dunkeh
More, please.	**Mehr, bitte.** mair bitteh
Less than that.	**Etwas weniger.** etvahs vay-neeg-er
That's fine.	**Das ist gut so.** dahs ist goot zo
OK.	**Gut.** goot
I won't take it, thank you.	**Ich nehme es nicht, danke.** ish nay-meh es nisht dunkeh
It's not right.	**Es ist nicht das Richtige.** es ist nisht dahs rish-teeg-eh
Thank you very much.	**Vielen Dank.** fee-len dunk

Do you have something . . .	**Haben Sie etwas …** h*ah*ben zee *e*tvahs
. . . better?	**Besseres?** *be*sser-es
. . . cheaper?	**Billigeres?** *bi*llig-er-es
. . . different?	**Anderes?** *u*nder-es
. . . larger?	**Größeres?** gr*e*rsser-es
. . . smaller?	**Kleineres?** kl*i*ner-es
At what time do you . . .	**Um wie viel Uhr …** oom *vee* feel *oo*r
. . . open?	**öffnen Sie?** *e*rffnen zee
. . . close?	**schließen Sie?** shl*ee*sen zee
Can I have a bag, please?	**Kann ich bitte eine Tragetasche haben?** kahn ish b*i*tteh *i*neh tr*ah*g-eh-tahsheh h*ah*ben
Can I have a receipt?	**Kann ich bitte eine Quittung haben?** kahn ish b*i*tteh *i*neh kv*i*tt-oong h*ah*ben
Do you take . . .	**Nehmen Sie …** n*ay*-men zee
. . . Canadian/English/American/ Australian money?	**kanadisches/englisches/ amerikanisches/australisches Geld?** kah-n*ah*-dishes/eng-lishes/ ameri-k*ah*-nishes/ow-strah- lishes ghelt
. . . traveller's checks?	**Reisechecks?** r*y*zeh-shecks
. . . credit cards?	**Kreditkarten?** kred*ee*t-karten
I'd like . . .	**Ich möchte …** ish m*e*rshteh
. . . one like that.	**eins davon.** *i*nes d*ah*-fon
. . . two like that.	**zwei davon.** tsv*y* d*ah*-fon

Shop Assistant

Can I help you?
Kann ich Ihnen behilflich sein?
kahn ish *ee*nen ba-h*i*lf-lish zine

What would you like?
Was darf es sein?
vahs darf es zine

Will that be all?
Kommt noch etwas dazu?
kohmt nohk *e*tvahs dah-ts*oo*

Is that all?
Ist das alles?
ist dahs *a*lles

Anything else?
Sonst noch etwas?
z*oh*nst nohk *e*tvahs

Would you like that wrapped?
Soll ich es einwickeln?
zohl ish es *i*ne-vickeln

Sorry, none left.
Leider ausverkauft.
l*i*der *o*ws-fair-kowft

We don't have any.
Wir haben keine.
veer h*a*hben k*i*neh

We don't have any more.
Wir haben keine mehr.
veer h*a*hben k*i*neh mair

How many do you want?
Wie viele möchten Sie?
v*ee* feeleh m*e*rshten zee

How much do you want?
Wie viel möchten Sie?
v*ee* feel m*e*rshten zee

Is that enough?
Ist das genug?
ist dahs ga-n*oo*k

Shopping for Food

Bread

Essential Information

- For finding a bakery, see "Asking Directions," p. 8.
- Here are key words to look for.

Bäckerei	Bakery
Bäcker	Baker
Brot	Bread

- Most supermarkets and general stores sell bread.
- Bakeries are open from 7:30 a.m. to 12:30 p.m. and from 2:30 p.m. to 6:30 p.m. on weekdays. On Saturdays they close at lunchtime. Many bakeries will be open on Sunday mornings from 10:00 a.m. to noon and close one afternoon during the week, usually on Wednesdays.

What to Say

Some bread, please.	**Brot, bitte.** brote b*i*tteh
A loaf (like that).	**Ein Brot (wie das da).** ine brote (vee d*ah*s dah)
A large one.	**Ein großes.** ine gr*oh*sses
A small one.	**Ein kleines.** ine kl*i*ne-es
A bread roll.	**Ein Brötchen.** ine br*e*rt-shen
A bread roll. (Bavaria, Austria)	**Eine Semmel.** *i*neh zemmel
A croissant.	**Ein Hörnchen.** ine h*e*rn-shen
Bread.	**Brot.** brote
Sliced bread.	**Geschnittenes Brot.** ga-shn*i*tten-es br*o*te
White bread.	**Weißbrot.** v*i*ce-brote
Rye bread.	**Graubrot.** gr*a*-oo-brote
Pumpernickel bread.	**Schwarzbrot.** shv*a*rts-brote

Whole grain bread.	**Vollkornbrot.**
	foll-korn-brote
Two loaves.	**Zwei Brote.**
	tsvy brote-eh
Four bread rolls.	**Vier Brötchen.**
	feer brert-shen
Four croissants.	**Vier Hörnchen.**
	feer hern-shen

Cakes

Essential Information

• The following are key words to look for.

Bäckerei	Bread and cake shop
Konditorei	Cake shop, often with a tearoom in the back
Café or Kaffeehaus	In Austria: a place to buy cakes and have a drink at a table, usually in the afternoon. See also "Ordering a Drink," p. 62.

• For finding a cake shop, see "Asking for Directions," p. 8.

What to Say

The type of cakes you find in the shops varies slightly from region to region, but the following are some of the most common.

jelly-filled doughnut	**der Berliner**
	dair ber-leener
almond flakes on a thin cake with a chocolate base	**der Florentiner**
	dair flor-en-teener
Black Forest cake	**die Schwarzwälder Kirschtorte**
	dee shvarts-velder keersh-torteh
glazed fruit on a sponge cake base	**die Obsttorte**
	dee ohbst-torteh
flaky pastry filled with apples, nuts, and raisins	**der Apfelstrudel**
	dair ahpfel-shtroodel
round pastry filled with pudding and covered with chocolate	**der Mohrenkopf**
	dair moren-kohpf
cheesecake	**der Käsekuchen**
	dair kaizeh-kooken
rich Viennese chocolate cake with jam	**die Sachertorte**
	dee zahker-torteh

Madeira cake	**der Sandkuchen**
	dair zunt-kooken
cream cake	**die Sahnetorte**
	dee zah-neh-torteh
cream cake sprinkled with flaky almonds and honey	**der Bienenstich**
	dair beenen-shtish

You usually buy individual pastries by number.

Two doughnuts, please.	**Zwei Berliner, bitte.**
	tsvy ber-leener bitteh

You buy large cakes by the slice.

One slice of fruit tart.	**Ein Stück Obsttorte.**
	ine shtook ohbst-torteh
Two slices of Madeira cake.	**Zwei Stück Sandkuchen.**
	tsvy shtook zunt-kooken

You may also want to say:

With whipped cream, please.	**Mit Sahne, bitte.**
	mit zah-ne bitteh

For other essential expressions, see "Shop Talk," p. 41.

Ice Cream and Sweets

Essential Information

- Look for the following key words.

Eis	Ice cream
Eisdiele	Ice-cream parlor
Eiscafé	Ice-cream parlor, tearoom
Süßwarenladen	Sweet shop
Konditorei	Cake shop

- The best known ice-cream brands are the following.

Langnese
Schöller
Dr. Oetker
Jopa

- Prepacked sweets are available in general stores and supermarkets.

What to Say

A . . . ice cream, please.	**Ein ... -eis, bitte.**
	ine ... ice bitteh
. . . caramel . . .	**Karamel**

	kahrah-mel
. . . chocolate . . .	**Schokoladen**
	shohko-*lah*den
. . . lemon . . .	**Zitronen**
	tsee-tronen
. . . raspberry . . .	**Himbeer**
	h*i*m-bear
. . . strawberry . . .	**Erdbeer**
	*ai*rt-bear
. . . vanilla . . .	**Vanille**
	Vah-n*i*l-yeh

At the Table

A single portion.	**Eine kleine Portion.**
	*i*neh kly-neh por-tsee-*oh*n
Two single portions.	**Zwei kleine Portionen.**
	tsv*y* kly-neh por-tsee-onen
A double portion.	**Eine große Portion.**
	*i*neh grohsseh por-tsee-*oh*n
Two double portions.	**Zwei große Portionen.**
	tsv*y* grohsseh por-tsee-onen
A mixed ice cream . . .	**Ein gemischtes Eis ...**
	ine ga-m*i*shtes ice
. . . with/without whipped cream.	**mit/ohne Sahne.**
	mit/*oh*neh z*ah*neh

Over the Counter

A cone . . .	**Ein Hörnchen ...**
	ine h*er*n-shen
A cup . . .	**Einen Becher ...**
	*i*nen besher
. . . with two scoops.	**mit zwei Kugeln.**
	mit tsv*y* k*oo*g-eln
. . . with three scoops.	**mit drei Kugeln.**
	mit dr*y* k*oo*g-eln
(60 cents') worth of ice cream.	**Ein Eis zu (sechzig).**
	*i*ne *i*ce tsoo (zek-tsig)
A packet of . . .	**Eine Packung ...**
	*i*neh p*ah*ck-oong ...
100 grams of . . .	**Hundert Gramm ...**
	h*oo*ndert grahm
200 grams of . . .	**Zweihundert Gramm ...**
	tsv*y*-hoondert grahm

. . . candy.	**Bonbons.** bong-bongs
. . . chocolates.	**Pralinen.** pra-*lee*nen
. . . mints.	**Pfefferminzbonbons.** pfeffer-m*i*nts-bong-bongs
. . . toffee.	**Karamelbonbons.** kahrahm*e*l-bong-bongs
A lollipop.	**Einen Dauerlutscher.** *i*nen *dow*er-lootsher

For other essential expressions, see "Shop Talk," p. 41.

In the Supermarket

Essential Information

- The following are key words to look for or use (see also "Asking Directions," p. 8).

Supermarkt	Supermarket
Selbstbedienungsladen	Corner self-service
Lebensmittelgeschäft	General food store

- Here are key instructions on signs in a shop.

Eingang	Entrance
Kein Eingang	No entry
Ausgang	Exit
Kein Ausgang	No exit
Kasse	Checkout
Schnellkasse	Express checkout up to five items

- Large supermarkets are open all day from 8:00 a.m. to 6:30 p.m. The smaller corner shops usually close at lunchtime, from 12:30 p.m. to 2:30 p.m.

- For nonfood items, see "Replacing Equipment," p. 39.

- Usually, there's no need to say anything in a supermarket, but ask if you can't see what you want.

What to Say

Excuse me, please.	**Entschuldigen Sie, bitte.** ent-*shool*-dig-en zee b*i*tteh
Where is . . .	**Wo ist ...** *vo* ist

. . . the bread?	**das Brot?**
	dahs brote
. . . the butter?	**die Butter?**
	dee booter
. . . the cheese?	**der Käse?**
	dair kay-zeh
. . . the chocolate?	**die Schokolade?**
	dee shohko-lahdeh
. . . the coffee?	**der Kaffee?**
	dair kahffeh
. . . the cooking oil?	**das Speiseöl?**
	dahs shpyzeh-erl
. . . the fresh fish section?	**die Fischabteilung?**
	dee fish-uptile-oong
. . . the fruit?	**das Obst?**
	dahs ohbst
. . . the jam?	**die Marmelade?**
	dee marmeh-lahdeh
. . . the meat?	**das Fleisch?**
	dahs flysh
. . . the milk?	**die Milch?**
	dee milsh
. . . the mineral water?	**das Mineralwasser?**
	dahs minerahl-vahsser
. . . the salt?	**das Salz?**
	dahs zahlts
. . . the sugar?	**der Zucker?**
	dair tsoocker
. . . the tea?	**der Tee?**
	dair tay
. . . the vegetable section?	**die Gemüseabteilung?**
	dee ga-moozeh-uptieloong
. . . the vinegar?	**der Essig?**
	dair essik
. . . the wine?	**der Wein?**
	dair vine
. . . the yogurt?	**der Joghurt?**
	dair yohg-oort
Where are . . .	**Wo sind ...**
	vo zint
. . . the biscuits/cookies?	**die Kekse?**
	dee cake-seh
. . . the potato chips?	**die Kartoffelchips?**
	dee kar-tohffel-ships

. . . the eggs?	**die Eier?**
	dee *eye*-er
. . . the frozen foods?	**die Tiefkühlwaren?**
	dee *teef*-kool-vahren
. . . the fruit juices?	**die Fruchtsäfte?**
	dee *frookt*-zefteh
. . . the pastas?	**die Teigwaren?**
	dee *tike*-vahren
. . . the soft drinks?	**die alkoholfreien Getränke?**
	dee ahlkohole-fry-en ga-*trenk*eh
. . . the sweets?	**die Süßigkeiten?**
	dee *zoo*-sick-kiten
. . . the canned vegetables?	**die Gemüsekonserven?**
	dee ga-*moo*zeh-cone-zairven
. . . the canned foods?	**die Konserven?**
	dee cone-*zai*rven

For other essential expressions, see "Shop Talk," p. 41.

Picnic Food

Essential Information

- The following are key words to look for.

Delikatessengeschäft	Delicatessen
Feinkostgeschäft	Delicatessen
Metzgerei	Butcher shop
Schlachterei	Butcher shop

Here's a guide to the amount of prepared salad to buy.

- 2–3 ounces/70 grams of prepared salad per person, if eaten as an appetizer to a substantial meal.
- 3–4 ounces/100 grams of prepared salad per person, if eaten as the main part of a picnic-style meal.

What to Say

A slice of . . .	**Eine Scheibe . . .**
	*i*neh *shy*-beh
Two slices of . . .	**Zwei Scheiben . . .**
	tsvy *shy*-ben
. . . cooked ham.	**gekochten Schinken.**
	ga-*koh*kten *shi*nken

. . . raw cured ham.	**rohen Schinken.** *roh*-en sh*in*ken
. . . roast beef.	**Rostbraten.** *rohst*-brahten
. . . cervelat.	**Zervelatwurst.** zair-vel*ah*t-voorst
. . . tongue sausage.	**Zungenwurst.** ts*oo*gen-voorst
. . . garlic sausage.	**Knoblauchwurst.** knope-lowk-voorst
. . . salami.	**Salami.** zahl*ah*-mi
100 grams of . . .	**Hundert Gramm ...** h*oo*ndert grahm
150 grams of . . .	**Hundertfünfzig Gramm ...** h*oo*ndert-f*oo*nf-tsick grahm
200 grams of . . .	**Zweihundert Gramm ...** tsvy-h*oo*ndert grahm
300 grams of . . .	**Dreihundert Gramm ...** dry-h*oo*ndert grahm
. . . herring salad.	**Heringsalat.** h*air*ing-zahl*ah*t
. . . egg salad.	**Eiersalat.** *eye*-er-zahl*ah*t
. . . chicken salad.	**Geflügelsalat.** ga-fl*oo*g-el-zahl*ah*t
. . . potato salad.	**Kartoffelsalat.** kart*oh*ffel-zahl*ah*t
. . . tomato salad.	**Tomatensalat.** tohm*ah*ten-zahl*ah*t

You might also like to try some of the following.

a pizza	**eine Pizza** *i*neh p*i*zza
some goose liver pâté	**ein Stück Gänseleberpastete** ine shtook ghen-zeh-laber- pahst*ai*teh
some luncheon sausage	**ein Stück Fleischwurst** ine shtook fl*y*sh-voorst
white salted herring	**einen Matjeshering** *i*nen m*ah*t-yes-h*air*ing
a spicy, thick meatball (often eaten cold)	**eine Frikadelle** *i*neh frika-d*e*ll*eh*

a smoked eel	**einen Räucheraal** *i*nen roy-sher-ahl
two frankfurters	**ein paar Frankfurter** ine par fr*u*nk-foorter
a Bavarian sausage	**eine Weißwurst** *i*neh vice-voorst
a spicy sausage from Thuringia	**eine Thüringer Bratwurst** *i*neh tooring-er br*a*ht-voorst
shredded meat and cheese salad	**einen Elsässer Wurstsalat** *i*nen *e*l-zesser voorst-zahl*a*ht
some meatloaf	**ein Stück Leberkäse** ine shtook l*a*ber-kay-zeh
a sausage roll	**eine Wurstpastete** *i*neh voorst-pahst*ai*teh
a vol-au-vent	**eine Königin-Pastete** *i*neh kerneeg-in past*ai*teh
a chicken vol-au-vent	**eine Geflügelpastete** *i*neh ga-floog-el-pahst*ai*teh
soft cream cheese with herbs	**einen Kräuterquark** *i*nen kr*o*yter-kvark
mild cheese	**Tilsiter** t*i*l-zit-er
cheese with caraway seeds	**Kümmelkäse** k*oo*mmel-kaizeh
sharp, roll-shaped cheese	**einen Harzer Roller** *i*nen h*a*rtser roller
Swiss cheese	**Emmentaler** *e*mmen-tahler
Dutch cheese	**Gouda** g*o*wdah
Camembert/Brie	**Camembert/Brie** c*a*hmem-bair/br*ee*

For other essential expressions, see "Shop Talk," p. 41.

Fruit and Vegetables

Essential Information

• Look for the following key words.

Obst	Fruit
Gemüse	Vegetables
Obst und Gemüsehändler	Fruit and vegetable shop

- If possible, buy fruit and vegetables at a market, where they are cheaper and fresher than in the shops.
- Weight guide: one kilo of potatoes serves six people.

What to Say

1 pound (½ kilo) of . . .	**Ein Pfund (ein halbes Kilo) ...** ine pfoont (ine hallbes kilo)
1 kilo of . . .	**Ein Kilo ...** ine kilo
2 kilos of . . .	**Zwei Kilo ...** tsvy kilo
. . . apples.	**Äpfel.** epfel
. . . bananas.	**Bananen.** bahnah-nen
. . . cherries.	**Kirschen.** keer-shen
. . . grapes.	**Weintrauben.** vine-trah-ooben
. . . oranges.	**Apfelsinen.** ahpfel-zeenen
. . . pears.	**Birnen.** beer-nen
. . . peaches.	**Pfirsiche.** pfeer-zisheh
. . . plums.	**Pflaumen.** pfla-oomen
. . . strawberries.	**Erdbeeren.** aird-bairen
A pineapple, please.	**Eine Ananas, bitte.** ineh ah-nahnahs bitteh
A grapefruit.	**Eine Pampelmuse.** ineh pumpel-moozeh
A melon.	**Eine Melone.** ineh melone-eh
A watermelon.	**Eine Wassermelone.** ineh vahsser-melone-eh
½ pound of . . .	**Ein halbes Pfund ...** ine hallbes pfoont
1 pound of . . .	**Ein Pfund ...** ine pfoont
1 kilo of . . .	**Ein Kilo ...** ine kilo

3 pounds of . . .	**Drei Pfund ...** dry pfoont
2 kilos of . . .	**Zwei Kilo ...** tsvy kilo
. . . artichokes.	**Artischocken.** arti-shoken
. . . avocados.	**Avocados.** ahvo-kahdose
. . . carrots.	**Karotten.** kahrohten
. . . eggplants.	**Auberginen.** ober-jeenen
. . . green beans.	**grüne Bohnen.** grooneh bone-en
. . . leeks.	**Lauch/Porree.** lowk/por-ray
. . . mushrooms.	**Pilze.** pil-tseh
. . . onions.	**Zwiebeln.** tsvee-beln
. . . peas.	**Erbsen.** airpsen
. . . potatoes.	**Kartoffeln.** kar-tohffeln
. . . red cabbage.	**Rotkohl.** rote-kole
. . . spinach.	**Spinat.** shpee-naht
. . . tomatoes.	**Tomaten.** tohmahten
. . . zucchini.	**Zucchini.** tsoo-kini
A bunch of . . .	**Ein Bund ...** ine boont
. . . parsley.	**Petersilie.** pater-zeel-yeh
. . . radishes.	**Radieschen.** rah-dees-shen
. . . shallots.	**Schalotten.** shah-loten
A head of garlic.	**Knoblauch.** knope-la-ook

A lettuce.	**Einen Kopfsalat.**
	*i*nen *ko*hpf-zahlaht
A cauliflower.	**Einen Blumenkohl.**
	*i*nen bloomen-kole
A cabbage.	**Einen Weißkohl.**
	*i*nen vice-kole
A cucumber.	**Eine Salatgurke.**
	*i*neh zahl*ah*t-goorkeh
Like that, please.	**So eine, bitte.**
	zo *i*neh *bi*tteh

The following fruits and vegetables may not be familiar to you.

type of plum used for a plum tart	**Zwetschge**
	tsv*e*tsh-ge
small sour variety of cherry	**Sauerkirsche**
	z*ow*-er keersheh
small, yellow plum	**Reneklode**
	reneh-klodeh
mandarin orange	**Mandarine**
	mandah-r*ee*neh
seedless, small tangerine	**Klementine**
	klemen-t*ee*neh
vegetable similar to turnip in shape and taste	**Kohlrabi**
	kole-r*ah*bee
fennel, crunchy vegetable with aniseed flavor	**Fenchel**
	fenshel
Savoy cabbage	**Wirsingkohl**
	v*ee*r-zing-kole

For other essential expressions, see "Shop Talk," p. 41.

Meat

Essential Information

- Look for the following key words.

Metzgerei	Butcher shop
Fleischerei	Butcher shop
Schlachterei	Butcher shop
Metzger	Butcher
Fleischer	Butcher
Schlachter	Butcher

- Weight guide: 4–6 ounces/125–200 grams of meat per person.

Beef **Rind**

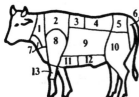

1 Hals	8 Schulter
2 Zungenstück	9 Querrippe
(Zungengrat)	(Zwerchrippe)
3 Hohe Rippe	10 Blume (Rose)
4 Filet (Lende)	11 Brust
5 Hüfte	12 Bauch (Nabel)
6 Schwanzstück	13 Beinfleisch
7 Stich	

Veal **Kalb**

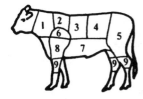

1 Hals
2 Nacken
3 Kotelett
4 Nierenbraten
5 Keule (Schlegel)
6 Blatt
7 Brust
8 Schulter
9 Haxe

Pork **Schwein**

1 Keule
2 Rücken
3 Nacken (Kamm)
4 Bauch
5 Schulter (Vorderschinken)
6 Eisbein

Mutton **Hammel**

1 Keule
2 Rücken
3 Hals
4 Brust
5 Schulter

- The figures can help you make sense of labels on counters and supermarket displays, as well as decide which cut or roast to have. Translations are often unhelpful, and you won't need to say the German word.
- You will find that lamb and especially mutton are less popular in Germany. The butcher's display will tell you what's available.

What to Say

For a roast, choose the type of meat and then say how many people it is for.

Some beef, please.	**Rindfleisch, bitte.** rint-flysh bitteh
Some lamb.	**Lamm.** lahm
Some mutton.	**Hammelfleisch.** hahmmel-flysh
Some pork.	**Schweinefleisch.** shvine-eh-flysh
Some veal.	**Kalbfleisch.** kahlp-flysh
A roast . . .	**Einen Braten ...** inen brahten
. . . for two people.	**für zwei Personen.** foor tsvy per-zonen
. . . for four people.	**für vier Personen.** foor feer per-zonen

To order steak, liver, or kidneys, say the following.

Some steak, please.	**Steak, bitte.** steak bitteh
Some liver.	**Leber.** laber
Some kidneys.	**Nieren.** neeren
Some sausages.	**Würstchen.** voorst-shen
Some minced meat.	**Hackfleisch.** hahck-flysh
. . . for three people.	**für drei Personen.** foor dry per-zonen
. . . for five people.	**für fünf Personen.** foor foonf per-zonen

To order chops, say the following.

Two veal cutlets, please.	**Zwei Kalbsschnitzel, bitte.**
	tsvy kahlps-shnitsel bitteh
Three pork chops.	**Drei Schweinekoteletts.**
	dry shvine-eh-coatlets
Five lamb chops.	**Fünf Lammkoteletts.**
	foonf lahm-coatlets

You may also want the following.

A chicken.	**Ein Huhn.**
	ine hoon
A tongue.	**Eine Zunge.**
	ineh tsoong-eh

For other essential expressions, see "Shop Talk," p. 41.

Please can you . . .	**Können Sie ... bitte?**
	kernnen zee ... bitteh
. . . mince it?	**es durch den Fleischwolf drehen**
	es doorsh dehn flysh-volf dray-en
. . . dice it?	**es in kleine Stücke schneiden**
	es in kly-neh shtook-eh shnyden
. . . trim the fat?	**das Fett abschneiden**
	dahs fett up-shnyden

Fish

Essential Information

- Look for the following signs.

Fischgeschäft	Fish shop
Fischabteilung	Fish section in the food department of a larger store

- Look also for **Nordsee**—a fresh fish chain that also sells smoked and marinated specialties, as well as snack meals.

- Shellfish (**Meeresfrüchte**) is quite rare in Germany.

- Large markets usually have fresh fish stands.

- Weight guide: a minimum of 8 ounces/250 grams of fish with bones serves one person. Use the following table as a guide.

½ kilo/500 grams	for two people
1 kilo	for four people
1½ kilos	for six people

What to Say

Purchase large fish and small shellfish by weight.

1 pound (½ kilo) of . . .	**Ein Pfund (ein halbes Kilo) ...** ine pfoont (ine hahlbes kilo)
1 kilo of . . .	**Ein Kilo ...** ine kilo
3 pounds (1½ kilos) of . . .	**Drei Pfund ...** dry pfoont
. . . carp.	**Karpfen.** karp-fen
. . . cod.	**Kabeljau.** kahbel-yow
. . . haddock.	**Schellfisch.** shell-fish
. . . halibut.	**Heilbutt.** hile-boot
. . . mussels.	**Muscheln.** moosheln
. . . pike.	**Hecht.** hesht
. . . prawns.	**Krabben.** krahben
. . . red sea bass.	**Rotbarsch.** rote-barsh
. . . shrimp.	**Garnelen.** gar-nay-len
. . . shrimp. (N. Germany)	**Granat.** grah-naht
. . . turbot.	**Steinbutt.** shtine-boot

Some large fish can be purchased by the slice.

One slice of . . .	**Ein Stück ...** ine shtook
Two slices of . . .	**Zwei Stück ...** tsvy shtook
Six slices of . . .	**Sechs Stück ...** zex shtook
. . . cod.	**Kabeljau.** kahbel-yow
. . . haddock.	**Schellfisch.** shell-fish

. . . halibut.	**Heilbutt.**
	h*i*le-boot
Two slices of salmon.	**Zwei Scheiben Lachs.**
	tsv*y* shy-ben lahks

For some shellfish and pan-fry fish, specify the number you want.

A crab, please.	**Einen Krebs, bitte.**
	*i*nen kreps b*i*tteh
A crayfish.	**Eine Languste.**
	*i*neh lung*oo*st-eh
A flounder.	**Eine Scholle.**
	*i*neh shole-eh
A herring.	**Einen Hering.**
	*i*nen h*ai*r-ing
A lobster.	**Einen Hummer.**
	*i*nen h*oo*mmer
A mackerel.	**Eine Makrele.**
	*i*neh mahk-*rai*leh
A sole.	**Eine Seezungė.**
	*i*neh z*ay*-tsoong-eh
A trout.	**Eine Forelle.**
	*i*neh forell-eh

For other essential expressions, see "Shop Talk," p. 41.

Please can you . . .	**Können Sie, bitte …**
	k*e*rnen zee b*i*tteh
. . . take the heads off?	**Kopf und Schwanz entfernen?**
	k*o*hpf oont shv*ah*nts ent-f*ai*rnen
. . . clean them?	**den Fisch ausnehmen?**
	dehn fish *ows*-nay-men
. . . fillet them?	**den Fisch in Scheiben schneiden?**
	dehn fish in shy-ben shny-den

Eating and Drinking Out
Ordering a Drink
Essential Information

- Here are the places to ask for (see also "Asking Directions," p. 8).

  Ein Café
  Eine Wirtschaft   A type of pub
  Eine Weinstube   A wine bar

- By law, the price list of drinks (**Getränkekarte**) must be displayed outside or in the window.

- There is waiter service in all cafés, pubs, and wine bars. In a pub, you can also drink at the bar if you wish, which is cheaper.

- A service charge of 10%–15% is almost always included on the bill (**Bedienung inbegriffen**), but it is customary to leave some additional small change.

- Cafés serve nonalcoholic and alcoholic drinks and are normally open all day.

What to Say

I'll have . . . , please.	**Ich hätte gern ..., bitte.** ish hetteh gairn ... bitteh
. . . a black coffee . . .	**einen schwarzen Kaffee** inen shvar-tsen kahffeh
. . . a coffee with cream . . .	**einen Kaffee mit Sahne** inen kahffeh mit zahneh
. . . a tea . . .	**einen Tee** inen tay
. . . with milk . . .	**mit Milch** mit milsh
. . . with lemon . . .	**mit Zitrone** mit tsee-trone-eh
. . . a glass of milk . . .	**ein Glas Milch** ine glahss milsh
. . . two glasses of milk . . .	**zwei Glas Milch** tsvy glahss milsh
. . . a hot chocolate . . .	**eine heiße Schokolade** ineh hysseh shohko-lahdeh
. . . a mineral water . . .	**ein Mineralwasser** ine minerahl-vahsser

. . . a lemonade . . .	**eine Limonade** *i*neh lim-o-n*ah*deh
. . . a Coca-Cola . . .	**eine (Coca-) Cola** *i*neh (coca) cola
. . . an orangeade . . .	**einen Orangensprudel** *i*nen o-r*u*ng-shen-shpr*oo*del
. . . a fresh orange juice . . .	**einen frischen Orangensaft** *i*nen fr*i*shen o-r*u*ng-shen-zahft
. . . a grape juice . . .	**einen Traubensaft** *i*nen tr*ah*-*oo*ben-zahft
. . . an apple juice . . .	**einen Apfelsaft** *i*nen *ah*pfel-zahft
. . . a beer . . .	**ein Bier** ine b*ee*r
. . . a draught beer . . .	**ein Bier vom Fass** ine b*ee*r fom f*ah*ss
. . . a light ale . . .	**ein helles Bier** ine h*e*ll-es b*ee*r
. . . a lager . . .	**ein Pilsener** ine p*i*l-zen-er
. . . a bitter . . .	**ein Altbier** ine *ah*lt-beer
. . . a brown ale . . .	**ein dunkles Bier** ine d*oo*nkles b*ee*r
. . . a small galss . . .	**ein Kleines** ine kly-nes
A glass of . . .	**Ein Glas . . .** ine gl*a*ss
Two glasses of . . .	**Zwei Glas . . .** tsvy glahss
. . . red wine.	**Rotwein.** r*o*te-vine
. . . white wine.	**Weißwein.** v*i*ce-vine
. . . rosé wine.	**Rosé.** r*o*zay
. . . dry wine.	**herben** h*ai*r-ben
. . . sweet wine.	**süßen** s*oo*ssen
A bottle of . . .	**Eine Flasche . . .** *i*neh fl*ah*sheh
. . . sparkling wine.	**Schaumwein.** sha-*oo*m-vine

. . . champagne. (German)	**Sekt.** zekt
. . . champagne. (French)	**Champagner.** shahm-*pah*nyer
A whisky . . .	**Einen Whisky ...** *i*nen *vi*sky
. . . with ice.	**mit Eis.** mit *i*ce
. . . with water.	**mit Wasser.** mit *vah*sser
. . . with soda.	**mit Soda.** mit *zo*da
A gin . . .	**Einen Gin ...** *i*nen gin
. . . with tonic.	**mit Tonik.** mit *toh*nic
. . . with bitter lemon.	**mit Bitter Lemon.** mit *bi*tter *le*mon
A brandy/cognac.	**Einen Weinbrand/Kognak.** *i*nen *vi*ne-brahnt/*cone*-yuck
A martini.	**Einen Martini.** *i*nen mar*ti*ni
A sherry.	**Einen Sherry.** *i*nen sherry

Here are some local drinks you may like to try.

a strong spirit distilled from grain	**ein Schnaps** ine shn*ah*ps
light Berlin ale with raspberry juice	**eine Berliner Weiße** *i*neh ber-*lee*ner *vi*ce-eh
raspberry brandy	**ein Himbeergeist** ine *hi*m-bear-gyst
strong Munich beers	**ein Doppelbock/Märzen** ine d*oh*ppel-bohck/m*ai*r-tsen
a bitter with bits of pineapple	**eine Altbierbowle** *i*neh *ah*lt-beer-boleh
Black Forest brandy distilled from cherries	**ein Kirschwasser** ine k*ee*rsh-vahsser
hot, diluted rum with sugar	**ein Grog** ine gr*o*ke
mulled wine	**ein Glühwein** ine gl*oo*-vine
dark, sweet malt beer	**ein Malzbier** ine m*a*lts-beer

eggnog	**ein Eierlikör** ine *eye*-er-leek*er*

Other essential expressions include the following.

Waitress!	**Frau Kellnerin!** frow kell-ner-in
Waiter!	**Herr Ober!** h*air* o-ber
The bill, please.	**Die Rechnung, bitte.** dee resh-noong b*i*tteh
How much does that come to?	**Wie viel macht das insgesamt?** vee feel mahkt dahs ins-ga-z*ah*mt
Is service included?	**Ist Bedienung inbegriffen?** ist ba-d*ee*n-oong *i*n-ba-griffen
Where is the restroom, please?	**Wo sind die Toiletten, bitte?** *vo* zint dee twah-letten, b*i*tteh

Ordering a Snack

Essential Information

- Look for any of these places.

Schnellimbiss	Snack bar
Imbissstube	Snack bar
Bratwurststand	Sausage stand
Hähnchen-Grill	Chicken takeout; **Wienerwald** is a popular chain
Nordsee	A fish shop and takeout chain found in larger towns

- All of these places also sell soft drinks, canned or bottled beer, tea, coffee, and so on.
- You will find the names of snacks on signs in the window or on the sidewalk signs.
- For cakes, see p. 46. For ice cream, see p. 47. For picnic food, see p. 51.

What to Say

I'll have . . ., please.	**Ich hätte gern ..., bitte.** ish hetteh gairn ... b*i*tteh
. . . a cheese sandwich/roll . . .	**ein Käsebrot/Käsebrötchen** ine k*ai*zeh-brote/k*ai*zeh-brertshen
. . . a ham sandwich/roll . . .	**ein Schinkenbrot/**

	Schinkenbrötchen
	ine shinken-brote/
	shinken-brertshen
. . . a roll with fish . . .	**ein Fischbrötchen**
	ine fish-brertshen
. . . an omelet . . .	**ein Omelett**
	ine ohmelet
. . . with mushrooms . . .	**mit Pilzen**
	mit pil-tsen
. . . with diced ham . . .	**mit Schinken**
	mit shinken

Here are some other snacks you might like to try.

a bratwurst	**eine Bratwurst**
	ineh braht-voorst
a large frankfurter	**eine Bockwurst**
	ineh bohck-voorst
a grilled sausage topped with curry sauce and ketchup	**eine Currywurst**
	ineh curry-voorst
half a (roast) chicken	**ein halbes Hähnchen**
	ine hahlbes hain-shen
a hamburger steak	**ein Deutsches Beefsteak**
	ine doyt-shes beefsteak
two fried eggs	**ein paar Spiegeleier**
	ine par shpeeg-el-eye-er
goulash	**eine Gulaschsuppe**
	ineh goulahsh-zoopeh

You may want to add one of the following to your order.

with bread, please	**mit Brot, bitte**
	mit brote bitteh
with French fries	**mit Pommes frites**
	mit pome frit
with potato salad	**mit Kartoffelsalat**
	mit kar-tofel-zahlaht
with (fried) onions	**mit Zwiebeln**
	mit tsvee-beln
with mustard	**mit Senf**
	mit zenf
with ketchup	**mit Ketchup**
	mit ketchup
with mayonnaise	**mit Mayonnaise**
	mit mayo-naizeh

For other essential expressions, see "Ordering a Drink," p. 62.

In a Restaurant

Essential Information

- The place to look for is **ein Restaurant** (see "Asking Directions," p. 8).
- You can eat at any of the following places.

Restaurant	
Hotel-Restaurant	
Gaststätte/Gasthof	
Rasthof	At highway rest areas
Bahnhofsbüfett	At train stations
Grillstube	
Café	Limited choice here

- By law, menus must be displayed outside or in the window. That is a very helpful way to judge if a place is right for you.
- Self-service restaurants are not unknown, but most places have waiter service.
- A service charge of 10%–15% is usually included in restaurant bills. But if you are satisfied with the service, you should leave some small change.
- Most restaurants offer small portions for children. Look for **Kinderteller** (children's portion) on the menu.
- Hot meals are served from 12:00 p.m. to 2:00 p.m. at lunchtime and from 6:00 p.m. to 9:00 p.m. or 10:00 p.m. at night. After that, many restaurants offer snacks for latecomers (soups, sausages, salads, etc.). Ask for the "small menu": **die kleine Karte** (dee kly-neh karteh).

What to Say

May I reserve a table?	**Kann ich einen Tisch reservieren lassen?** kahn ish *i*nen t*i*sh reser-veeren lahssen
I've reserved a table.	**Ich habe einen Tisch reservieren lassen.** ish h*a*hbeh *i*nen t*i*sh reser-veeren l*a*ssen
A table . . .	**Einen Tisch ...** *i*nen t*i*sh

. . . for one.	**für eine Person.** foor *i*neh per-*zone*
. . . for three.	**für drei Personen.** foor dry per-*zonen*
The à la carte menu, please.	**Die Speisekarte, bitte.** dee shpyzeh-karteh *bi*tteh
The fixed-price menu.	**Die Gedeckkarte.** dee ga-*deck*-karteh
The tourist menu.	**Das Touristenmenü.** dahs touristen-men*oo*
Today's special menu.	**Die Karte mit Tagesgedecken.** dee *k*arteh mit *t*ahg-es-ga-*d*ecken
What's this, please? [*point to menu*] The wine list.	**Was ist dies, bitte?** *v*ahs ist d*ee*s *bi*tteh **Die Weinkarte.** dee *v*ine-karteh
A carafe of wine, please.	**Eine Karaffe Wein, bitte.** *i*neh kah-*rah*ffeh *v*ine *bi*tteh
A quarter-liter (250 cc).	**Einen Viertelliter.** *i*nen *f*eer-tel-liter
A half-liter (500 cc).	**Einen halben Liter.** *i*nen *h*ahlben *l*iter
A glass.	**Ein Glas.** ine *gl*ahss
A bottle.	**Eine Flasche.** *i*neh *fl*ahsheh
A half-bottle.	**Eine halbe Flasche.** *i*neh *h*ahlbeh *fl*ahsheh
A liter.	**Einen Liter.** *i*nen *l*iter
Red/white/rosé/house wine.	**Rotwein/Weißwein/Rosé/ Hauswein.** rote-vine/vice-vine/rozay/ house-vine
Some more bread, please.	**Noch etwas Brot, bitte.** nohk *e*tvahs brote *bi*tteh
Some more wine.	**Noch etwas Wein.** nohk *e*tvahs *v*ine
Some oil.	**Etwas Öl.** *e*tvahs erl
Some vinegar.	**Etwas Essig.** *e*tvahs essick
Some salt.	**Etwas Salz.** *e*tvahs *z*ahlts

Some pepper.	**Etwas Pfeffer.**
	etvahs pf*e*ffer
Some water.	**Etwas Wasser.**
	etvahs v*a*hsser
How much does that come to?	**Wie viel macht das insgesamt?**
	v*ee* feel mahkt dahs ins-ga-z*a*hmt
Is service included?	**Ist Bedienung inbegriffen?**
	ist ba-d*ee*n-oong *i*n-ba-griffen
Where are the restrooms, please?	**Wo sind die Toiletten, bitte?**
	v*o* zint dee twah-letten b*i*tteh
Waitress!	**Frau Kellnerin!**
	fr*o*w kell-ner-in
Waiter!	**Herr Ober!**
	hair *o*-ber
The bill, please.	**Die Rechnung, bitte.**
	dee r*e*sh-noong b*i*tteh

Here are some key words for meal courses, as seen on some menus.

What have you got for . . .	**Was für ... haben Sie?**
	v*a*hs foor ... h*a*hben zee
. . . appetizers?	**Vorspeisen**
	for-shpyzen
. . . soup?	**Suppen**
	z*oo*ppen
. . . egg dishes?	**Eierspeisen**
	eye-er-shpyzen
. . . fish?	**Fischgerichte**
	f*i*sh-ga-risht-eh
. . . meat?	**Fleischgerichte**
	fl*y*sh-ga-risht-eh
. . . game?	**Wildgerichte**
	v*i*lt-ga-risht-eh
. . . fowl?	**Geflügelgerichte**
	ga-fl*oo*gel-ga-risht-eh
. . . vegetables?	**Gemüse**
	ga-m*oo*zeh
. . . cheese?	**Käse**
	k*a*y-zeh
. . . fruit?	**Obst**
	ohpst
. . . ice cream?	**Eis**
	ice
. . . dessert?	**Nachspeisen**
	n*a*hk-shpyzen

Understanding the Menu

- The main ingredients of most dishes are given on the following pages.

  Meat (p. 56)
  Fish (p. 59)
  Vegetables (p. 53)
  Fruit (p. 53)
  Dessert (p. 46)
  Ice cream (p. 47)

Together with the following list of cooking and menu terms, the ingredient lists should help you decode a menu.

- These cooking and menu terms are for understanding only; for this reason, no pronunciation guide is given.

Cooking and Menu Terms

angemacht	in a special dressing
Auflauf	soufflé
blau	steamed and served with butter
blutig	rare
Bouillon	broth, clear soup
Brat-	fried
-braten	roast
-brühe	broth
-brust	breast
Butter-	buttered
durchgebraten	well done
gebacken	baked
gedämpft	steamed
gedünstet (Austria)	steamed, stewed
gefüllt	stuffed
gegrillt	grilled
gekocht	boiled
in Gelee	jellied
gemischt	mixed
gepökelt	salted, pickled
geräuchert	smoked
gerieben	grated
geschmort	braised, stewed

gespickt	larded, smoked
halbdurch	medium
Hausfrauenart	with apple, sour cream, and onions
hausgemacht	homemade
Holländisch	with mayonnaise
Holstein	topped with fried egg, garnished with anchovies and vegetables
Jägerart	served in red wine sauce with mushrooms
-Kaltschale	chilled fruit soup
-Kompott	stewed fruit
Kraftbrühe	broth, beef consommé
Kräuter-	with herbs
mariniert	marinated
Meerrettich-	with horseradish
Müllerin	baked in butter, dressed with bread crumbs and egg
paniert	dressed with egg and bread crumbs
Pell-	boiled in the jacket
Petersilien-	with parsley
-püree	mashed
Rahm-	with cream
roh	raw
Röst-	fried
Sahne-	creamed
sauer	sour
Schlemmer-	for the gourmet
Schnitzel	escalope (of veal)
Senf-	with mustard
Soße	sauce
Sülz-	in aspic
süß	sweet
überbacken	au gratin
Zwiebel-	with onions

Ingredients and Other Helpful Menu Terms

Aalsuppe	eel soup, a specialty of Hamburg
Aufschnitt	sliced cold meat and sausages
Austern	oysters
Bauernomelett	bacon and onion omelette

Bierwurst	beer sausage
Birne Helene	vanilla ice cream with pear and hot chocolate sauce
Bismarckhering	soused herring with onions
Blutwurst	black pudding
Bockwurst	large frankfurter
Bratkartoffeln	fried potatoes
Bratwurst	bratwurst (with herbs)
Deutsches Beefsteak	hamburger steak
Eisbein	pig's knuckle
Ente	duck
Erbsensuppe	thick pea soup
Fasan	pheasant
Fleischkäse	type of meatloaf, sliced and fried
Forelle	trout
Frühlingssuppe	fresh vegetable soup
Gänseleberpastete	goose liver pâté
Gefrorenes	ice-cream specialties
Grünkohl	kale
Hackbraten	meatloaf
Kaiserschmarren	shredded pancake with raisins and almonds
Kartoffelpuffer	small potato-and-onion pancakes
Kasseler Rippenspeer	cured pork chops with mustard sauce
Klöße/Knödel	dumplings
Königsberger Klopse	meatballs in a white caper sauce
Kohlrouladen	cabbage stuffed with minced meat
Labskaus	pork and potato stew served with fried eggs and gherkins
Lachs	salmon
Leberknödelsuppe	soup with liver dumplings
Leberwurst	liver pâté
Linsensuppe	lentil soup
Matjeshering	young salted herring
Ochsenschwanzsuppe	oxtail soup
Ölsardinen	canned sardines
Paprikaschoten	bell peppers
Pfannkuchen	pancake
Pfirsich Melba	peaches with vanilla ice cream, whipped cream, raspberry syrup

Räucheraal	smoked eel
Rauchwurst	smoked sausage
Rehrücken	saddle of venison
Rollmops	pickled herring fillet, rolled around onion slices
Rosenkohl	brussels sprouts
Rösti	hashed brown potatoes
Röstkartoffeln	roast potatoes
Rote Beete	beets
Rotkraut	red cabbage
Russische Eier	hard-boiled eggs, with caper and mayonnaise dressing
Sardellen	anchovies
Sauerbraten	beef marinated in vinegar, sugar, and spices and then braised
Sauerkraut	pickled white cabbage
Schildkrötensuppe	turtle soup
Schinkenwurst	ham sausage
Schlachtplatte	assorted cold meat and sausages
Schweinhaxe	pig's knuckle
Serbische Bohnensuppe	spicy Serbian bean soup
Spargel	asparagus
Spätzle	southern German variety of pasta
Speck	bacon
Strammer Max	raw ham and fried eggs, served on rye bread
Truthahn	turkey
Weinbergschnecken	snails with garlic, herbs, and butter
Wienerschnitzel	veal escalope in bread crumbs

Health

Essential Information

- For details about reciprocal health agreements between your country and the country you are visiting, visit your local department of health office at least one month before leaving, or ask your travel agent.

- In addition, it is preferable to purchase a medical insurance policy through a travel agent, an insurance broker, or a travel organization.

- Take your own emergency first-aid kit with you.

- For minor health problems and treatment at a drugstore, see "General Shopping," p. 29.

- For finding the way to a doctor, dentist, drugstore, or Social Security office (for reimbursement), see "Asking Directions," p. 8.

- Once in Germany, Austria, or Switzerland, decide on a definite plan of action in case of serious illness: let a neighbor, the receptionist, or someone you see regularly know about your problem. You are then dependent on that person to help you obtain treatment.

- In an emergency, dial 110 for ambulance service.

- If you need a doctor, look for **Ärzte** in the telephone directory. Here are important signs to look for.

Praxis	Surgery
Erste Hilfe	First aid
Krankenhaus/Hospital	Hospital
Unfallstation	Emergency department of a hospital

What's the Matter?

I have a pain in my . . .	**Ich habe Schmerzen ...**
	ish h*ah*beh shm*ai*rts-en
. . . abdomen.	**im Unterleib.**
	im *oo*nter-lipe
. . . ankle.	**im Fußgelenk.**
	im f*oo*ss-ga-lenk
. . . arm.	**im Arm.**
	im *a*rm

. . . back.	**im Rücken.** im r*oo*cken
. . . bladder.	**an der Blase.** un dair bl*ah*-zeh
. . . bowels.	**im Darm.** im d*a*rm
. . . breast.	**in der Brust.** in dair br*oo*st
. . . chest.	**im Brustkorb.** im br*oo*st-korp
. . . ear.	**im Ohr.** im *o*r
. . . eye.	**im Auge.** im *owg*-eh
. . . foot.	**am Fuß.** um f*oo*ss
. . . head.	**im Kopf.** im k*o*hpf
. . . heel.	**an der Ferse.** un dair f*air*-zeh
. . . jaw.	**im Kiefer.** im k*ee*fer
. . . kidneys.	**an den Nieren.** un dehn n*ee*ren
. . . leg.	**im Bein.** im b*i*ne
. . . lung.	**in der Lunge.** in dair l*oo*ng-eh
. . . neck.	**im Genick.** im ga-n*i*ck
. . . penis.	**im Penis.** im p*ai*nis
. . . shoulder.	**in der Schulter.** in dair sh*oo*lter
. . . stomach.	**im Magen.** im m*ah*-ghen
. . . testicles.	**in den Hoden.** in dehn h*o*den
. . . throat.	**im Hals.** im h*ah*ls
. . . vagina.	**in der Vagina.** in dair v*ah*g-ee-nah
. . . wrist.	**im Handgelenk.** im h*u*nt-ga-lenk

I have a pain here. [point]	**Ich habe hier Schmerzen.** ish h*a*hbeh here shm*a*irts-en
I have a toothache.	**Ich habe Zahnschmerzen.** ish h*a*hbeh ts*a*hn-shm*a*irts-en
I have broken my dentures.	**Mein Gebiss ist zerbrochen.** mine ga-b*i*s ist tsair-br*o*ken
I have broken my glasses.	**Meine Brille ist zerbrochen.** m*i*neh br*i*lleh ist tsair-br*o*ken
I have lost . . .	**Ich habe ... verloren.** ish h*a*hbeh ... fair-l*o*ren
. . . my contact lenses.	**meine Kontaktlinsen** m*i*neh conet*a*hkt-lin-zen
. . . a filling.	**eine Füllung** *i*neh f*oo*loong
My child is ill.	**Mein Kind ist krank.** mine k*i*nt ist krunk
He/she has a pain in his/her . . .	**Er/sie hat Schmerzen ...** air/zee haht shm*a*irts-en
. . . ankle. [see list above]	**im Fußgelenk.** im f*oo*ss-ga-lenk

How Bad Is It?

I'm ill.	**Ich bin krank.** ish bin kr*u*nk
It's urgent.	**Es ist dringend.** es ist dr*i*ng-ent
It's serious.	**Es ist etwas Ernstes.** es ist *e*tvahs *ai*rnstes
It's not serious.	**Es ist nichts Ernstes.** es ist n*i*shts *ai*rnstes
It hurts.	**Es tut weh.** es toot v*ay*
It hurts a lot.	**Es tut sehr weh.** es toot z*ai*r vay
It doesn't hurt much.	**Es tut nicht sehr weh.** es toot n*i*sht zair vay
The pain occurs . . .	**Der Schmerz tritt ... auf.** dair shm*a*irts trit ... owf
. . . every quarter of an hour.	**alle Viertelstunde** *a*lleh f*ee*rtel-shtoondeh
. . . every half-hour.	**alle halbe Stunde** *a*lleh h*a*llbeh shtoondeh
. . . every hour.	**jede Stunde** y*ai*deh shtoondeh

. . . every day.	**jeden Tag** y*ai*den t*a*hk
. . . most of the time.	**fast ununterbrochen** fahst *oo*n-oonter-broken
I've had it for . . .	**Ich habe es seit . . .** ish h*a*hbeh es z*i*te
. . . one hour/one day.	**einer Stunde/einem Tag.** *i*ner sht*oo*ndeh/inem t*a*hk
. . . two hours/two days.	**zwei Stunden/zwei Tagen.** tsvy sht*oo*nden/tsvy t*a*hg-en
It's a . . .	**Es ist ein . . .** es ist ine
. . . sharp pain.	**stechender Schmerz.** sht*e*shen-der shmairts
. . . dull ache.	**dumpfer Schmerz.** d*oo*mpfer shmairts
. . . nagging pain.	**bohrender Schmerz.** boren-der shmairts
I feel dizzy/sick.	**Mir ist schwindlig/übel.** meer ist shv*i*ndlik/*oo*bel
I feel weak/feverish.	**Ich fühle mich schwach/fieberig.** ish f*oo*leh mish shv*a*hk/f*ee*b-rik

Are you already being treated for something else?

I take . . . regularly. [*show*]	**Ich nehme regelmäßig . . .** ish n*ay*-meh r*ai*g-el-mahsik
. . . this medicine	**dieses Medikament.** d*ee*zes medicahment
. . . these tablets	**diese Tabletten.** d*ee*zeh tahbletten
I have . . .	**Ich habe . . .** ish h*a*hbeh
. . . a heart condition.	**ein Herzleiden.** ine h*ai*rts-ly-den
. . . hemorrhoids.	**Hämorrhoiden.** hemorro-*ee*-den
. . . rheumatism.	**Rheuma.** r*oy*mah
I'm . . .	**Ich bin . . .** ish bin
. . . diabetic.	**Diabetiker.** dee-ah-b*e*ticker
. . . asthmatic.	**Asthmatiker.** ahst-m*a*h-ticker

. . . pregnant.	**schwanger.**
	shv*ah*nger
. . . allergic to (penicillin).	**allergisch gegen (Penicillin).**
	all*air*-gish g*ay*-gen (peni-tsee-l*ee*n)

Other Essential Expressions

Please can you help?	**Können Sie bitte helfen?**
	k*er*nen zee b*i*tteh helfen
A doctor, please.	**Einen Arzt, bitte.**
	*i*nen *a*rtst b*i*tteh
A dentist.	**Einen Zahnarzt.**
	*i*nen ts*ah*n-artst
I don't speak German.	**Ich spreche nicht Deutsch.**
	ish shpresheh nisht d*o*ytsh
What time does . . . arrive?	**Um wie viel Uhr kommt ... ?**
	oom *vee* feel *oo*r kohmt
. . . the doctor . . .	**der Arzt**
	dair *a*rtst
. . . the dentist . . .	**der Zahnarzt**
	dair ts*ah*n-artst.

Here are important things the doctor may tell you.

Take this . . .	**Nehmen Sie dies ...**
	n*ay*-men zee d*ee*s
. . . every day/hour.	**täglich/stündlich.**
	t*ai*k-lish/shtoont-lish
. . . twice/three times a day.	**zweimal/dreimal pro Tag.**
	tsvy-mahl/dry-mahl pro t*ah*k
Stay in bed.	**Bleiben Sie im Bett.**
	bly-ben zee im bet
Don't travel . . .	**Reisen Sie nicht ...**
	ryzen zee n*i*sht
. . . for . . . days/weeks.	**in den nächsten ... Tagen/Wochen.**
	in dehn neksten ... t*ah*g-en/
	voke-en
You must go to a hospital.	**Sie müssen ins Krankenhaus.**
	zee m*oo*ossen ins kr*u*nken-house

Problems: **Complaints, Loss, and Theft**

Essential Information

- If you have problems with . . .

    . . . camping facilities, see "Accommodations," p. 15.
    . . . your health, see "Health," p. 74.
    . . . household appliances, see "Replacing Equipment," p. 39.
    . . . a car, see "Car Travel," p. 88.

- If worse comes to worst, find the police station (if necessary, see "Asking Directions," p. 8).
- Look for the following signs.

Polizei	Police
Polizeiwache	Police station

- Ask for the **Fundbüro** (lost and found) if you are looking for lost items.
- If you lose your passport, go to your nearest consulate.
- In an emergency, dial 110 for the police and 112 for the fire department.

Complaints

I bought this . . .	**Ich habe dies ... gekauft.**
	ish h*a*hbeh dees ... ga-k*o*wft
. . . today.	**heute**
	h*o*y-teh
. . . yesterday.	**gestern**
	gh*e*stern
. . . on Monday.	**Montag**
	m*o*ne-tahk

For days of the week, see p. 112.

It's no good.	**Es ist nicht in Ordnung.**
	es ist n*i*sht in *o*rt-noong
Look.	**Sehen Sie.**
	z*a*y-en zee
Here. [*point*]	**Hier.**
	here

Can you . . .	**Können Sie ...**
	kernen zee
. . . change it?	**es umtauschen?**
	es oom-towshen
. . . mend it?	**es in Ordnung bringen?**
	es in ort-noong bringen
Here's the receipt.	**Hier ist der Kassenzettel.**
	here ist dair kahssen-tsettel
Can I have a refund?	**Kann ich das Geld zurückbekommen?**
	kahn ish dahs ghelt tsoo-rook-ba-komen
Can I see the manager?	**Kann ich den Geschäftsführer sprechen?**
	kahn ish dehn ga-shefts-foorer shprechen

Loss

See also the following section, "Theft." The lists are interchangeable.

I have lost . . .	**Ich habe ... verloren.**
	ish hahbeh ... fair-loren
. . . my bag.	**meine Handtasche**
	mineh hun-tahsheh
. . . my bracelet.	**mein Armband**
	mine arm-bunt
. . . my camera.	**meine Kamera**
	mineh kahmerah
. . . my car keys.	**meine Autoschlüssel**
	mineh owtoe-shloosel
. . . my vehicle registration papers.	**meinen Kraftfahrzeugschein**
	minen krahft-far-tsoyk-shine
. . . my driver's license.	**meinen Führerschein**
	minen foorer-shine
. . . my insurance card.	**meine Versicherungskarte**
	mineh fair-zisheroongs-karteh
. . . my jewelry.	**meinen Schmuck**
	minen shmoock
. . . my keys.	**meine Schlüssel**
	mineh shloosel
. . . everything!	**alle meine Sachen!**
	alleh mineh zahken

Theft

See also the preceding section, "Loss." The lists are interchangeable.

Someone has stolen . . .	**Man hat ... gestohlen.**
	mahn haht ... ga-shtolen
. . . my car.	**mein Auto**
	mine *ow*toe
. . . my car radio.	**mein Autoradio**
	mine *ow*toe-rahdio
. . . my money.	**mein Geld**
	mine ghelt
. . . my necklace.	**meine Halskette**
	m*i*neh h*ah*ls-ketteh
. . . my passport.	**meinen Pass**
	m*i*nen p*ah*ss
. . . my radio.	**mein Radio**
	mine r*ah*dio
. . . my tickets.	**meine Fahrkarten**
	m*i*neh far-karten
. . . my traveler's checks.	**meine Reiseschecks**
	m*i*neh ryzeh-shecks
. . . my wallet.	**meine Brieftasche**
	m*i*neh br*ee*f-tahsheh
. . . my watch.	**meine Uhr**
	m*i*neh *oo*r
. . . my luggage.	**mein Gepäck**
	mine ga-peck

Likely Reactions

Wait, please.	**Warten Sie, bitte.**
	v*a*rten zee b*i*tteh
When?	**Wann?**
	vahn
Where?	**Wo?**
	vo
Your name?	**Ihr Name?**
	eer n*ah*meh
Address?	**Adresse/Anschrift?**
	ah-dr*e*sseh/*u*n-shrift
I can't help you.	**Ich kann Ihnen nicht helfen.**
	ish kahn *ee*nen nisht h*e*lf-en
I'm not responsible for that.	**Ich bin dafür nicht zuständig.**
	ish bin dah*foo*r nisht ts*oo*-shtendik

The Post Office

Essential Information

- For finding a post office, see "Asking Directions," p. 8.
- Here are the key words to look for.

  Post
  Postamt
  Bundespost

- Look for this sign.
- To buy stamps, look for the words **Briefmarken** or **Postwertzeichen** on a post office counter.
- Some stationery stores and kiosks that sell postcards also sell stamps.
- Mailboxes in Germany, Switzerland, and Austria are yellow, but you may still find some blue ones in Austria. A red point on the mailbox indicates that it is emptied frequently, late at night (**Spätleerung**), and also on Sundays.
- Plain, stamped postcards and stamps can also be obtained from yellow vending machines located outside post offices or at the back of phone booths. Ask for **Briefmarken Automat** or look for the word **Wertzeichengeber**.
- For having your mail held through general delivery, you need to show your passport at the counter marked **Postlagernde Sendungen** in the main post office; a small fee is usually required.

What to Say

To Australia.	**Nach Australien.**
	nahk owstrah-lee-en

[*Hand the letters, cards, or packages over the counter.*]

To Canada, please.	**Nach Kanada, bitte.**
	nahk kah-nah-dah bitteh
To England, please.	**Nach England, bitte.**
	nahk eng-lant bitteh
To the United States.	**In die Vereinigten Staaten.**
	in dee ferine-nik-ten shtahten

For the names of other countries, see "Countries and Nationalities," p. 116.

How much is . . .	**Wie viel kostet …** *vee* feel *koh*stet …
. . . this package (to Canada)?	**dieses Paket (nach Kanada)?** *dee*zes pah-*ka*te (*nahk* kah- na-dah)
. . . a letter (to Australia)?	**ein Brief (nach Australien)?** ine breef (*nahk* owst*rah*-lee-en)
. . . a postcard (to England)?	**eine Postkarte (nach England)?** *ine*h post-*karte*h (*nahk* eng-lant)
Air mail.	**Luftpost.** *looft*-post
Surface mail.	**Normaler Tarif.** norm*ah*-ler tah-*reef*
One stamp, please.	**Eine Briefmarke, bitte.** *ine*h breef-*marke*h *bi*tteh
Two stamps.	**Zwei Briefmarken.** tsvy breef-*marke*n
One (50)-cent stamp.	**Eine Briefmarke zu (fünzig) Cent.** *ine*h breef-*marke*h tsoo (foonf-tsik) tsent
I'd like to send this overnight.	**Ich möchte dieses Express und über Nacht schicken.** ish m*e*rshteh d*ee*zes express oont oober-n*ah*kt sh*i*cken

Telephoning

Essential Information

- Public telephones (**Öffentlicher Fernsprecher**) are often yellow and take coins. Foreign calls can only be made from booths marked with a green disc and the words **International** or **Ausland**.

- To use a public telephone, lift the receiver, insert the money, and dial the telephone number (unused coins will be refunded).

- To call the United Kingdom, dial 0044; the code to the United States is 001.

- If you need an international code, dial **Auskunft** (Information) at 00118. They normally understand English.

- To call countries that cannot be dialed directly, go to a post office and write the country, town, and number you want on a piece of paper. Add **Mit Voranmeldung** if you want a person-to-person call or **R-Gespräch** if you want to reverse the charges.

- If you have trouble making a phone call, go to the post office and ask them to put the call through (see previous bullet).

- A cellular phone is a **Mobiltelefon** or **Handy**.

What to Say

Where can I make a telephone call?	**Wo kann ich telefonieren?** vo kahn ish tele-fohneeren
local/long-distance	**Ein Ortsgespräch/ein Auslandsgespräch** ine orts-ga-shpraish/ine ows-lunts-ga-shpraish
I'd like this number . . . [show number]	**Ich möchte diese Nummer ...** ish mershteh deezeh noomer
. . . in Australia.	**in Australien.** in ow-strah-lee-en
. . . in England.	**in England.** in eng-lunt
. . . in Canada.	**in Kanada.** in kah-nah-dah
. . . in the United States.	**in den Vereinigten Staaten.** in dehn ferine-nik-ten shtahten

For the names of other countries, see "Countries and Nationalities," p. 116.

Can you dial it for me, please?	**Können Sie für mich wählen, bitte?** kernnen zee foor mish vay-len bitteh
How much is it?	**Wie viel kostet es?** vee feel kohstet es
Hello!	**Hallo!** hullo
May I speak to . . . ?	**Kann ich mit … sprechen?** kahn ish mit … shpreshen
Extension . . .	**Apparat …** apparaht
I'm sorry, I don't speak German.	**Es tut mir leid, ich spreche nicht Deutsch.** es toot meer lite ish shpresheh nisht doytsh
Do you speak English?	**Sprechen Sie Englisch?** shpreshen zee eng-lish
Thank you, I'll call back.	**Danke, ich rufe wieder an.** dunkeh ish roofeh veeder ahn
Good-bye.	**Auf Wiederhören.** owf veeder-hern
What's your cell phone number?	**Was ist Ihre Mobiltelefonnummer?** vahs ist eehreh moh-beel-telefone-noomer

Likely Reactions

That's (4) euros (50).	**Das macht (vier) Euro (fünfzig).** dahs mahkt (feer) oy-roe (foonf-tsik)
Cabin number (3).	**Kabine Nummer (drei).** kahbeeneh noomer (dry)
Don't hang up.	**Bleiben Sie am Apparat.** blyben zee ahm appa-raht
I'm trying to connect you.	**Ich verbinde Sie.** ish fer-bin-deh zee
You're through.	**Hier ist Ihre Verbindung.** here ist eereh fer-bin-doong
There's a delay.	**Sie müssen warten.** zee moossen varten
I'll try again.	**Ich versuche es noch einmal.** ish fer-zookeh es nohk ine-mahl
My cell phone number is . . .	**Meine Mobiltelefonnummer ist …** mineh moh-beel-telefon-noomer ist

Cashing Checks and Changing Money

Essential Information

- For finding your way to a bank or a currency exchange, see "Asking Directions," p. 8.

- Here are key words to look for on buildings.

Bank	Bank
Sparkasse	Bank, savings bank
Wechselstube/Geldwechsel	Currency exchange

- Banks are normally open from 8:00 a.m. to 12:30 p.m. and from 2:30 p.m. to 4:00 p.m. on weekdays. On Thursdays they stay open until 5:30 p.m. They are closed on Saturdays and Sundays.

- Currency exchanges at border-crossing stations, airports, and larger railway stations are usually open outside of regular banking hours.

- Changing money or traveler's checks is usually a two-stage process. The formalities are completed at a desk called **Devisen**; you will then be sent to the **Kasse** (cashier) to get your money.

- To cash your checks that you regularly use at home, present your credit card where you see the **Eurocheck** sign. Write in English and have your passport handy.

- Automatic teller machines (**Geldautomat**) are found in many convenient locations. You may access funds from your U.S. bank at most ATMs, by using your ATM card.

What to Say

I'd like to cash . . .	**Ich möchte ... einlösen.**
	ish mershteh ... ine-lerzen
. . . this traveler's check.	**diesen Reisescheck**
	deezen ryzeh-sheck
. . . these traveler's checks.	**diese Reiseschecks**
	deezeh ryzeh-shecks
. . . this check.	**diesen Scheck**
	deezen sheck
I'd like to change this into euros.	**Ich möchte dies in Euro wechseln.**
	ish mershteh dees in oy-roe vexeln
Here's my passport.	**Hier ist mein Pass.**
	here ist mine pahss

Is there an ATM nearby?

Gibt es einen Geldautomaten in der Nähe?
geept es *i*nen ghelt-ow-toe-mahten in dair n*a*y-eh

The following expressions may be used for excursions into neighboring countries.

I'd like to change this . . .
[*show cash*]

Ich möchte dies ... wechseln.
ish m*e*rshteh dees ... v*e*xeln

. . . into euros.

in Euro
in *oy*-roe

. . . into Swiss francs.

in Schweizer Franken
in shv*y*tser fr*u*nken

What's the exchange rate?

Wie ist der Wechselkurs?
v*ee* ist dair v*e*xel-koors

Likely Reactions

Your passport, please.

Ihren Pass, bitte.
*ee*ren p*a*hss b*i*tteh

Sign here.

Unterschreiben Sie hier.
oonter-shr*y*ben zee h*e*re

Go to the cash desk.

Gehen Sie zur Kasse.
g*a*y-en zee tsoor k*a*hsseh

There's an ATM . . .

Es gibt einen Geldautomaten ...
es geept *i*nen ghelt-ow-to-mahten

. . . over there.

dort drüben.
dort dr*oo*ben

. . . next door.

gleich nebenan.
gl*y*she nay-ben-*ah*n

. . . one block away.

eine Straße von hier entfernt.
*i*neh shtr*a*hss-eh fon h*e*re ent-f*a*irnt

Car Travel

Essential Information

- To ask directions to a gas station or garage, see "Asking Directions," p. 8.
- If you need a self-service station, look for **Selbstbedienung** or **SB**.
- The following are the gasoline grades.

Benzin/Normal	Regular
Super	Premium
Diesel	
Motorradöl/Mehrbereichsöl	Two-stroke oil

- One gallon is about 3¾ liters (accurate enough up to 6 gallons).
- The minimum sale is around 5 liters (often less at self-service pumps).
- Gas stations can usually deal with minor mechanical problems. For major repairs, you have to find a garage (**Reparaturwerkstatt**).
- For road signs and warnings, see "Reference," p. 103.

What to Say

For numbers, see p. 108.

(Nine) liters of . . .	**(Neun) Liter ...** (noyn) liter
(Thirty) euros' worth . . .	**Für (dreißig) Euro ...** foor (dry-sik) oy-roe
. . . of regular.	**Normal.** nor-mahl
. . . of premium.	**Super.** zooper
. . . of diesel.	**Diesel.** deezel
Fill it up, please.	**Volltanken, bitte.** folltunken bitteh
Will you check . . .	**Bitte prüfen Sie ...** bitteh proofen zee
. . . the battery.	**die Batterie.** dee bahteree
. . . the oil.	**das Öl.** dahs erl
. . . the radiator.	**das Kühler.** dahs kool-vahsser

. . . the tires.	**die Reifen.**
	dee ryfen
I've run out of gasoline.	**Ich habe kein Benzin mehr.**
	ish hahbeh kine ben-tseen mair
Can I borrow a can, please?	**Können Sie mir einen Kanister leihen?**
	kernen zee meer inen kahsnister ly-en
My car has broken down.	**Ich habe eine Panne.**
	ish hahbeh ineh pahnneh
My car won't start.	**Mein Wagen springt nicht an.**
	mine vahg-en shprinkt nisht ahn
I've had an accident.	**Ich habe einen Unfall gehabt.**
	ish hahbeh inen oon-fahl ga-hapt
I've lost my car keys.	**Ich habe meine Autoschlüssel verloren.**
	ish hahbeh mine owtoe-shloosel fair-loren
My car is . . .	**Mein Wagen steht ...**
	mine vahg-en shtait
. . . one kilometer away.	**einen Kilometer von hier.**
	inen kilo-mahter fon here
. . . three kilometers away.	**drei Kilometer von hier.**
	dry kilo-mahter fon here
Can you help me, please?	**Können Sie mir bitte helfen?**
	kernnen zee meer bitteh helf-en
Do you do repairs?	**Machen Sie Reparaturen?**
	mahk-en zee reparah-tooren
I have a flat tire.	**Ich habe eine Reifenpanne.**
	ish hahbeh ineh ryfen-pahnneh
I have a broken windshield.	**Die Windschutzscheibe ist zerbrochen.**
	dee vint-shoots-shybeh ist tsair-brocken
I don't know what's wrong.	**Ich weiß nicht, woran es liegt.**
	ish vice nisht vorahn es leekt
I think the problem is here . . . [point]	**Ich glaube, es liegt hieran ...**
	ish gla-oobeh es leekt here-un
Can you . . .	**Können Sie ...**
	kernen zee
. . . repair it?	**es reparieren?**
	es repareeren
. . . come and look?	**es sich ansehen?**
	es zish un-zay-en

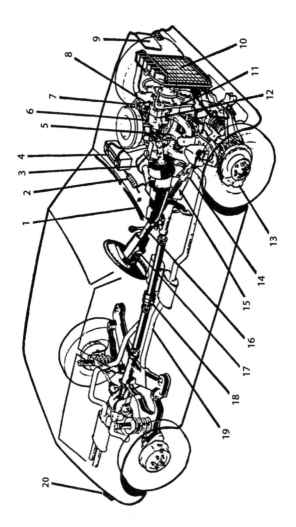

1 windshield wipers	**Scheibenwischer** shyben-visher	11 fan belt	**Keilriemen** kile-reemen
2 fuses	**Sicherungen** zisher-oon-gen	12 generator	**Lichtmaschine** lisht-mahsheeneh
3 heater	**Heizung** hy-tsoong	13 brakes	**Bremsen** brem-zen
4 battery	**Batterie** bahteree	14 clutch	**Kupplung** koop-loong
5 engine	**Motor** mo-tore	15 gear box	**Getriebe(block)** ga-treebe(block)
6 fuel pump	**Benzinpumpe** ben-tseen-poompeh	16 steering	**Lenkung** lenk-oong
7 starter motor	**Anlasser** un-lahsser	17 ignition	**Zündung** tsoon-doong
8 carburetor	**Vergaser** fair-*gahzer*	18 transmission	**(Schalt-) Getriebe** (shalt) ga-treebeh
9 lights	**Scheinwerfer** shine-vairfer	19 exhaust	**Auspuff** ows-poof
10 radiator	**Kühler** kooler	20 turn signals	**Blinker** blinker

. . . estimate the cost?	**einen Kostenvoranschlag machen?** *i*nen kohsten-for-unshlahk m*ah*k-en
. . . write it down?	**es aufschreiben?** es *ow*f-shryben
How long will the repair take?	**Wie lange wird die Reparatur dauern?** vee l*u*ngeh veert dee reparah-t*oo*r dowern
When will the car be ready?	**Wann wird der Wagen fertig sein?** v*ah*n veert dair v*ah*g-en f*air*-tik zine
Can I see the bill?	**Kann ich die Rechnung sehen?** kahn ish dee r*esh*-noong z*ay*en
This is my insurance card.	**Hier ist meine Versicherungskarte.** here ist m*i*neh fair-z*i*sheroongs-karteh

Renting a Car

Can I rent a car?	**Kann ich einen Wagen mieten?** kahn ish *i*nen v*ah*g-en m*ee*ten
I need a car . . .	**Ich brauche einen Wagen ...** ish br*ow*keh inen v*ah*g-en
. . . for two people.	**für zwei Personen.** foor tsv*y* per-z*o*nen
. . . for five people.	**für fünf Personen.** foor f*oo*nf per-z*o*nen
. . . for one day.	**für einen Tag.** foor *i*nen t*ah*k
. . . for five days.	**für fünf Tage.** foor f*oo*nf t*ah*g-eh
. . . for a week.	**für eine Woche.** foor *i*neh v*o*ke-eh
Can you write down . . .	**Können Sie mir ... aufschreiben?** k*er*nnen zee meer ... *ow*f-shryben
. . . the deposit to pay?	**die Kautionssumme** dee kow-tsee-*o*ns-zoommeh
. . . the charge per kilometer?	**die Gebühr pro Kilometer** dahs ga-b*oo*r pro kilo-m*a*ter
. . . the daily charge?	**die Gebühr pro Tag** das gab*oo*r pro t*ah*k
. . . the cost of insurance?	**die Versicherungskosten** dee fair-z*i*sheroongs-k*o*hsten

Can I leave it in (Hamburg)?	**Kann ich ihn in (Hamburg) abliefern?** kahn ish een in (hum-boorg) up-leefern
What documents do I need?	**Was für Unterlagen brauche ich?** vahs foor oonter-lahg-en browkeh ish

Likely Reactions

We don't do repairs.	**Wir machen keine Reparaturen.** veer mahk-en kineh reparah-tooren
Where's your car?	**Wo steht Ihr Wagen?** vo shtait eer vahg-en
What make is it?	**Was für ein Wagen ist es?** vahs foor ine vahg-en ist es
Come back tomorrow/on Monday.	**Kommen Sie morgen/Montag wieder.** komen zee morgen/mone-tahk veeder

For days of the week, see p. 112.

We don't rent cars.	**Wir vermieten keine Wagen.** veer fair-meeten kineh vahg-en
Your driver's license, please.	**Ihren Führerschein, bitte.** eeren foorer-shine bitteh
The mileage is unlimited.	**Die Kilometerzahl ist unbegrenzt.** dee kilo-mater-tsahl ist oon-ba-grentst

Public Transportation

Essential Information

- For asking directions to the bus station, a bus stop, a streetcar stop, the train station, or a taxi stand, see "Asking Directions," p. 8.
- Remember that lining up for buses is unheard of!
- To get a taxi, you usually have to call the local **Taxizentrale** (taxi center) or go to a taxi stand. Hailing a taxi is less common and doesn't always work.
- Here are the different kinds of trains.

TEE	Trans Europe Express—luxury high-speed train with first class only
InterCity Express (ICE)/ Schnellzug/D-Zug	Long-distance trains, often between countries, stopping only at central train stations
Eilzug	Medium-distance, internal train, stopping only at bigger towns
Personenzug	Slow local trains, stopping at all stations
Nahverkehrszug	Local train, often to the suburbs

- Here are signs to look for. See also "Reference," p. 103.

Fahrkarten	Tickets, ticket office
Eingang	Entrance
Ausgang	Exit
Verboten	Forbidden
Gleis	Platform, track
Bahnsteig	Platform
Bahnhofsmission	Travelers' aid office
Auskunft	Information, information office
DB	Initials for German railways
Gepäckaufbewahrung	Baggage room
Bushaltestelle	Bus stop
Abfahrt	Timetable—for departures
Ankunft	Timetable—for arrivals
Gepäckabfertigung/ Gepäckannahme	Luggage office/forwarding office

- To buy a train ticket, go to the ticket office inside the train station. When traveling by bus or train, you usually pay as you board. When traveling by subway (**U-Bahn**), you buy your ticket from an automatic machine at the station. This also applies to trolleys in the larger cities where each trolley stop has a ticket machine. In most German cities, you can purchase a ticket that is interchangeable between streetcars, subways, and buses, going in one direction. (These tickets often can be bought at tobacco shops.) You can also buy a pass for a specified number of days; ask for a **Touristen-Fahrkarte** (tooristen-far-karteh) at a main train station ticket office.

What to Say

Where does the train for (Bonn) leave from?	**Auf welchem Gleis fährt der Zug nach (Bonn) ab?** owf velshem glise fairt dair tsook nahk (bone) up
At what time does the train leave for (Bonn)?	**Wann fährt der Zug nach (Bonn) ab?** vahn fairt dair tsook nahk (bone) up
At what time does the train arrive in Bonn?	**Wann kommt der Zug in (Bonn) an?** vahn kohmt dair tsook in (bone) ahn
Is this the train for (Bonn)?	**Ist dies der Zug nach (Bonn)?** ist dees dair tsook nahk (bone)
Where does the bus for (Cologne) leave from?	**Wo fährt der Bus nach (Köln) ab?** vo fairt dair boos nahk (kerln) up
At what time does the bus leave for (Cologne)?	**Wann fährt der Bus nach (Köln) ab?** vahn fairt dair boos nahk (kerln) up
At what time does the bus arrive at (Cologne)?	**Wann kommt der Bus in (Köln) an?** vahn kohmt dair boos in (kerln) ahn
Is this the bus for (Cologne)?	**Ist dies der Bus nach (Köln)?** ist dees dair boos nahk (kerln)
Do I have to change?	**Muss ich umsteigen?** moos ish oom-shtyg-en
Where does . . . leave from?	**Wo fährt ... ab?** vo fairt ... up
. . . the bus . . .	**der Bus** dair boos
. . . the train . . .	**der Zug** dair tsook

. . . the subway . . .	**die U-Bahn** dee *oo*-bahn
. . . for the airport . . .	**zum Flughafen** tsoom *flook*-hahfen
. . . for the cathedral . . .	**zur Kathedrale/zum Dom** tsoor kah-teh-dr*ah*leh/ tsoom dome
. . . for the beach . . .	**zum Strand** tsoom shtr*u*nt
. . . for the marketplace . . .	**zum Marktplatz** tsoom m*a*rkt-plahts
. . . for the railway station . . .	**zum Bahnhof** tsoom b*ah*n-hohf
. . . for the town center . . .	**zur Stadtmitte** tsoor sht*ah*t-mitteh
. . . for the town hall . . .	**zum Rathaus** tsoom r*ah*t-house
. . . for St. John's church . . .	**zur Johanneskirche** tsoor yo-h*ah*nes-keersheh
. . . for the swimming pool . . .	**zum Schwimmbad** tsoom sh*v*imm-baht
Is this . . .	**Ist dies ...** ist d*ee*s
. . . the bus for the marketplace?	**der Bus zum Marktplatz?** dair b*oo*s tsoom m*a*rkt-plahts
. . . the streetcar for the railway station?	**die Straßenbahn zum Bahnhof?** dee shtr*ah*ssen-bahn tsoom b*ah*n-hohf
Where can I get a taxi?	**Wo kann ich ein Taxi bekommen?** vo kahn ish ine t*ah*xi ba-komen
Can you tell me where to get off, please?	**Können Sie mir bitte sagen, wann ich aussteigen muss?** k*e*rnen zee meer b*i*tteh z*ah*g-en vahn ish *ow*s-shtyg-en moos
Can I reserve a seat?	**Kann ich einen Sitzplatz reservieren?** k*ah*n ish *i*nen z*i*ts-plahts rehserveeren
A one-way ticket.	**Eine einfache Fahrt.** *i*neh *i*ne-fahk-eh f*a*rt
A round-trip ticket.	**Eine Rückfahrkarte.** *i*neh r*oo*k-far-karteh
First class.	**Erster Klasse.** *a*irster kl*ah*sseh

Second class.	**Zweiter Klasse.** tsvy-ter klahsseh
One adult . . .	**Ein Erwachsener ...** ine air-vahksen-er
Two adults . . .	**Zwei Erwachsene ...** tsvy air-vahksen-eh
. . . and one child.	**und ein Kind.** oont ine kint
. . . and two children.	**und zwei Kinder.** oont tsvy kin-der
How much is it?	**Wie viel kostet das?** vee feel kohstet dahs

Likely Reactions

Over there.	**Dort drüben.** dort drooben
Here.	**Hier.** here
Platform (1).	**Gleis/Bahnsteig (Eins).** glice/bahn-shtyk (ines)
At (4) o'clock.	**Um (vier) Uhr.** oom (feer) oor

For telling times, see "Time," p. 110.

Change at (Hanover).	**Steigen Sie in (Hannover) um.** shtyg-en zee in (hahn-ofer) oom
Change at (the town hall).	**Steigen Sie am (Rathaus) um.** shtyg-en zee um (raht-house) oom
This is your stop.	**Hier müssen Sie aussteigen.** here moossen zee ows-shtyg-en
There's only first class.	**Es gibt nur erste Klasse.** es geept noor airsteh klahsseh
There's an extra fee.	**Sie müssen Zuschlag zahlen.** zee moossen tsoo-shlahk tsahlen

Leisure and Entertainment

Essential Information

- For asking directions to a place of entertainment, see "Asking Directions," p. 8.
- For telling time, see "Time," p. 110.
- For important signs, see "Reference," p. 103.

- In the more popular seaside resorts, you must pay to go on the beach (**Kurtaxe**) and to rent a **Strandkorb** (see picture).
- Smoking is generally forbidden in theaters and movie theaters. In some large cities, however, there are special movie theaters for smokers (often called **Smoky**) where you likely will have to pay more for the privilege of being free to smoke.
- It is customary to leave your coat at the coatroom in theaters.

What to Say

At what time does . . . open?	**Um wie viel Uhr wird ... geöffnet?** oom *vee* feel oor veert ... ga-*erff*net
. . .the art gallery . . .	**die Kunstgalerie** dee *koonst*-gahler*ee*
. . . the botanical garden . . .	**der botanische Garten** dair bo*tah*-nisheh *gar*ten
. . . the movie theater . . .	**das Kino** dahs *kee*-no
. . . the concert hall . . .	**der Konzertsaal** dair cone-ts*air*t-zahl
. . . the disco . . .	**die Diskothek** dee disco-*take*
. . . the museum . . .	**das Museum** dahs moo-z*ay*-oom
. . . the nightclub . . .	**der Nachtklub** dair *nahkt*-kloop
. . . the sports stadium . . .	**das Stadion** dahs sht*ah*-dee-ohn
. . . the swimming pool . . .	**das Schwimmbad** dahs shv*imm*-baht

. . . the theater . . .	**das Theater** dahs tay-*ah*ter
. . . the zoo . . .	**der Zoo** dair tsoe
At what time does . . . close?	**Um wie viel Uhr schließt . . .** oom *vee* feel oor shl*ee*st
. . . the art gallery . . .	**die Kunstgalerie?** dee k*oo*nst-gahler*ee*
At what time does . . . start?	**Um wie viel Uhr beginnt . . .** oom *vee* feel oor ba-gh*i*nnt
. . . the cabaret . . .	**das Kabarett?** dahs kahbarett
. . . the concert . . .	**das Konzert?** dahs cone-ts*air*t
. . . the film . . .	**der Film?** dair f*i*lm
. . . the match . . .	**das Spiel?** dahs shp*ee*l
. . . the play . . .	**das Stück?** dahs sht*oo*k
. . . the race . . .	**das Rennen?** dahs rennen
How much is it . . .	**Wie viel kostet es . . .** *vee* feel k*o*hstet es
. . . for an adult?	**für einen Erwachsenen?** foor *i*nen air-v*ah*ksen-en
. . . for a child?	**für ein Kind?** foor ine k*i*nt
Two adults, please. [*State price, if there's a choice*]	**Zwei Erwachsene, bitte.** tsv*y* air-v*ah*ksen-eh b*i*tteh
Three children, please.	**Drei Kinder, bitte.** dry k*i*n-der b*i*tteh
Parquet/first tier	**Parkett/erster Rang** parkett/*ai*rster rung
Do you have . . .	**Haben Sie . . .** h*ah*ben zee
. . . a program?	**ein Programm?** ine pro-gr*ah*m
. . . a guidebook?	**einen Führer?** *i*nen foorer
Where's the restroom, please?	**Wo sind die Toiletten, bitte?** *vo* zint dee twah-letten b*i*tteh
Where's the cloakroom?	**Wo ist die Garderobe?** *vo* ist dee gardeh-robeh

I would like lessons in . . .	**Ich möchte Unterricht nehmen im ...** ish mershteh oonter-risht naymen im
. . . skiing.	**Skifahren.** shee-fahren
. . . sailing.	**Segeln.** zaygeln
. . . waterskiing.	**Wasserskifahren.** vahsser-shee-fahren
. . . windsurfing.	**Windsurfen.** vind-surfen
Can I rent . . .	**Kann ich ... leihen?** kahn ish ... ly-en
. . . some skis?	**Skier** shee-er
. . . some ski boots?	**Skistiefel** shee-shteefel
. . . a boat?	**ein Boot** ine bote
. . . a fishing rod?	**eine Angel** ineh ung-el
. . . a beach chair?	**einen Strandkorb** inen shtrahnt-chorb
. . . the necessary equipment?	**die nötige Ausrüstung** dee nertig-eh ows-roostoong
How much is it . . .	**Wie viel kostet es ...** vee feel kohstet es
. . . per day/per hour?	**pro Tag/pro Stunde?** pro tahk/pro shtoondeh
Do I need a permit?	**Brauche ich einen Erlaubnisschein?** browkeh ish inen erlowp-nis-shine

Asking If Things Are Allowed

Essential Information

- To ask if something is allowed, use the German expression **Kann man ...?** ("May one . . . ?")
- The question **Kann man hier rauchen?** represents all of the following English variations.

  May one smoke here?
  May we smoke here?
  May I smoke here?
  Can one smoke here?
  Can I smoke here?
  Can we smoke here?
  Is it possible to smoke here?

- To save space, only the first English version, "May one . . . ?" is given in the following list.

What to Say

Excuse me, please.	**Entschuldigen Sie, bitte.** ent-sh*oo*l-dig-en zee b*i*tteh
May one . . .	**Kann man ...** k*a*hn mahn
. . . camp here?	**hier zelten?** here ts*e*lt-en
. . . come in?	**hereinkommen?** hair-*i*ne-komen
. . . dance here?	**hier tanzen?** here t*a*hntsen
. . . fish here?	**hier angeln?** here *u*ng-eln
. . . get a drink here?	**hier etwas zu trinken bekommen?** here *e*tvahs tsoo tr*i*nken ba-komen
. . . get out this way?	**hier hinausgehen?** here hin*ow*s-gay-en
. . . get something to eat here?	**hier etwas zu essen bekommen?** here *e*tvahs tsoo *e*ssen ba-komen
. . . leave one's things here?	**seine Sachen hier lassen?** z*i*neh z*a*hk-en here lahssen
. . . look around?	**sich umsehen?** zish *oo*m-zay-en

... park here?

hier parken?
here parken

... picnic here?

hier picknicken?
here pick-nicken

... sit here?

sich hier hinsetzen?
zish here hin-zetsen

... smoke here?

hier rauchen?
here rowken

... swim here?

hier baden?
here bahden

... take photos here?

hier fotografieren?
here fotograhf-eeren

... telephone here?

hier telefonieren?
here telefone-eeren

... wait here?

hier warten?
here varten

Likely Reactions

Yes, certainly.

Ja, gern(e).
yah gairn(eh)

Help yourself.

Ja, bitte.
yah bitteh

I think so.

Ich glaube ja.
ish gla-oobeh yah

Of course.

Natürlich.
nah-toor-lish

Yes, but be careful.

Ja, aber seien Sie vorsichtig.
yah ahber zy-en zee for-zishtik

No, certainly not.

Nein, auf keinen Fall.
nine owf kinen fahll

I don't think so.

Ich glaube nicht.
ish gla-oobeh nisht

Not normally.

Normalerweise nicht.
nor-mahler-vyzeh nisht

No, sorry.

Nein, tut mir leid.
nine toot meer lite

Reference

Public Notices

Signs for Drivers, Pedestrians, Travelers, Shoppers, and Overnight Guests

Abfahrt	Departure
Achtung	Caution
Ankunft	Arrivals
Anlieger frei	Access to residents only
Anmeldefreie waren	Nothing to declare
Anmeldepflichtige waren	Goods to declare
Anmeldung	Reception
... Auf eigene Gefahr	. . . at one's own risk
Aufzug	Elevator
Ausfahrt	Exit (from highway)
Ausgang	Exit
Auskunft	Information office
Ausverkauf	Sale, clearance sale
Ausverkauft	Sold out, full house
Autobahn	Highway
Bad	Bathroom
Baden verboten	No bathing
Bahnsteig	Platform
Bahnübergang	Level crossing
Baustelle	Building site
Bedarfshaltestelle	Bus stop on request
Besetzt	Occupied (toilet); full (bus)
Betreten verboten	No trespassing
Betriebsferien	Closed for holidays
Bewachter Parkplatz	Supervised parking place
Bitte klingeln	Ring (bell)
Bitte klopfen	Knock (door)
Bitte nicht stören	Do not disturb
Blaue Zone	Restricted parking zone
Damen	Ladies
Drücken	Push
Durchfahrt verboten	No through traffic
Durchgangsverkehr	Through traffic
Duschen	Showers

Einbahnstraße	One-way street
Einfahrt	Entrance to highway
Eingang	Entrance
Einordnen	Get in line
Einstieg vorn/hinten	Enter at the front/at the rear
Eintritt frei	Admission free
Einwurf	Slot, put in . . .
Ende (der Autobahn)	Highway ends
Engstelle	Road narrows
Entwerter	Ticket-stamping machine
Erdgeschoss	First floor
Erfrischungen	Refreshments
Erste Hilfe	First aid
Etage (erste, zweite, dritte)	Floor (first, second, third)
Fahrkartenschalter	Ticket office
Feiertags geschlossen	Closed on holidays
Fernsprecher	Public telephone
Feuermelder	Fire alarm
Frei	Vacant (toilet)
Freibad	Outdoor pool
Fremdenführer	Tour guide
Frostschaden	Road damaged by frost
Fundbüro	Lost and found
Fußgängerzone	Pedestrian zone
Gebühren	Fees, charges
Gefahr	Danger
Gefährliche Kurve	Dangerous curve
Gefährliche Strömungen	Dangerous currents
Gegenverkehr	Two-way traffic
Geöffnet	Open
Gepäckaufbewahrung	Baggage room
Gepäckträger	Porter
Geschlossen	Closed
Geschwindigkeitsgrenze	Speed limit
Gleis	Platform
Halt	Halt, stop
Heiß	Hot (tap)
Herren	Gentlemen
Höchstgeschwindigkeit	Maximum speed
Hochgarage	Multilevel parking garage
Hupen verboten	Honking is prohibited

Kalt	Cold (tap)
Kasse	Checkout
Kein Durchgang für Fußgänger	No pedestrians
Kein Trinkwasser	Not for drinking
Kein Zutritt	No entry
Krankenhaus	Hospital
Kreuzung	Intersection
Kundendienst	Customer service
Kurvenreiche Strecke	Winding road
Langsam fahren	Drive slowly, slow down
Lawinengefahr	Avalanche area
Lebensgefahr	Danger of death
Leerung	Collection (mail)
Licht einschalten	Lights on
Liegewagen	Couchette
Münzeneinwurf	Coin slot
Münzrückgabe	Coin return
Nicht berühren	Do not touch
Nichtraucher	Nonsmoking (compartment)
Notausgang	Emergency exit
Notbremse	Emergency brake
Öffentliche Toiletten	Public restrooms
Öffnungszeiten	Opening hours
Parken nur mit Parkscheiben	Park at meters only
Parken verboten	No parking
Parkplatz	Parking lot
Parterre	Ground floor
Polizei	Police
Privatgrundstück	Private property
Radweg	Bike path
Radweg Kreuzt	Bike crossing
Rauchen verboten	No smoking
Raucher	Smoking allowed
Rechts fahren	Keep right
Reserviert	Reserved
Rolltreppe	Escalator
Ruhetag	Closed all day
Rutschgefahr bei Nässe	Slippery surface in damp weather
Sackgasse	Dead end
Schlafwagen	Sleeping car, sleeper

Schlechte Fahrbahn	Rough road surface
Schließfächer	Luggage lockers
Schlussverkauf	(Seasonal) sale
Schnelldienst	Fast service
Schule	School
Seitenstreifen nicht befahrbar	Soft shoulders
Selbstbedienung	Self-service
Sonderangebot	Special offer
Spätvorstellung	Late showing
Speisewagen	Dining car
Sprechstunden	Office hours
Stehplätze	Standing room
Steinschlag	Falling rock
Straßenarbeiten	Roadwork
Straßenglätte	Slippery road
Tiefgarage	Underground parking garage
Tiefparterre	Basement, lower ground floor
Toiletten	Toilets
Trinkwasser	Drinking water
U-Bahn	Subway
Überholen verboten	Passing prohibited
Umleitung	Detour
Unbefugten ist das Betreten verboten	Trespassers will be prosecuted
Unbeschrankter Bahnübergang	Unguarded train crossing
Verboten	Forbidden
Verkehrsampeln	Traffic lights
Vorfahrt beachten	Yield
Vorsicht, bissiger Hund	Beware of dog
Vorsicht vor den Zügen	Watch out for trains
Wartesaal	Waiting room
Werktags geöffnet	Open on workdays
Ziehen	Pull
Zimmer frei	Vacancies
Zimmer zu vermieten	Room to rent
Zoll	Customs
Zutritt verboten	No admission
Zu verkaufen	For sale
Zu vermieten	For hire, for rent

Abbreviations

ACS	**Automobilclub der Schweiz**	Automobile Association of Switzerland
ADAC	**Allgemeiner Deutscher Automobilclub**	General Automobile Association of Germany
Adr	**Adresse**	address
AG	**Aktiengesellschaft**	joint-stock company, corporation
AOK	**Allgemeine Ortskrankenkasse**	local public health insurance office
AvD	**Automobilclub von Deutschland**	Automobile Club of Germany
B	**Bundesstraße**	federal road
Bayr	**Bayrisch**	Bavarian
BP	**Bundespost**	German postal service
BRD	**Bundesrepublik Deustchland**	Federal Republic of Germany
C	**Celsius**	Celsius
DB	**Deutsche Bahn**	German (Federal) Rail
DCC	**Deutscher Camping-Club**	German Camping Club
DM	**Deutsche Mark**	German mark
DRK	**Deutsches Rotes Kreuz**	German Red Cross
DSG	**Deutsche Service-Gesellschaft der Bahn**	German Sleeping Car Company
€	**Euro**	euro
GmbH	**Gesellschaft mit beschränkter Haftung**	limited liability company
Hbf	**Hauptbahnhof**	main train station
JH	**Jugendherberge**	youth hostel
km	**Kilometer**	kilometer
LKW	**Lastkraftwagen**	truck
m	**Meter**	meter
Min	**Minute**	minute
MWSt	**Mehrwertsteuer**	value-added tax
nachm	**nachmittags**	in the afternoon
ÖAMTC	**Österreichischer Automobil-, Motorrad- und Touring Club**	Austrian Automobile, Motorcycle, and Touring Club

ÖBB	**Österreichische Bundesbahnen**	Austrian (Federal) Railway
Pf(g)	**Pfennig**	pfennig
PKW	**Personenkraftwagen**	car
Pl	**Platz**	(town) square, plaza
Rp	**Rappen**	Swiss centime
SB	**Selbstbedienung**	self-service
SBB	**Schweizerische Bundesbahnen**	Swiss (Federal) Railway
St	**Stock**	floor, story
Stck	**Stück**	piece, item
Str	**Straße**	street
tägl	**täglich**	daily
TCS	**Touring Club Schweiz**	Swiss Touring Club
U-Bahn (or U)	**Untergrundbahn**	subway
vorm	**vormittags**	in the morning
WC	**Wasser-Klosett**	toilet, restroom

Numbers

Cardinal Numbers

0	**null**	nool
1	**eins**	ines
2	**zwei**	tsvy
3	**drei**	dry
4	**vier**	feer
5	**fünf**	foonf
6	**sechs**	zex
7	**sieben**	zeeben
8	**acht**	ahkt
9	**neun**	noyn
10	**zehn**	tsain
11	**elf**	elf
12	**zwölf**	tsverlf
13	**dreizehn**	dry-tsain
14	**vierzehn**	feer-tsain
15	**fünfzehn**	foonf-tsain
16	**sechzehn**	zek-tsain
17	**siebzehn**	zeep-tsain

18	**achtzehn**	*ah*k-tsain
19	**neunzehn**	noyn-tsain
20	**zwanzig**	tsv*ah*n-tsik
21	**einundzwanzig**	*i*ne-oont-tsvahn-tsik
22	**zweiundzwanzig**	tsv*y*-oont-tsvahn-tsik
23	**dreiundzwanzig**	dry-oont-tsvahn-tsik
24	**vierundzwanzig**	feer-oont-tsvahn-tsik
25	**fünfundzwanzig**	foonf-oont-tsvahn-tsik
30	**dreißig**	dry-sik
35	**fünfunddreißig**	foonf-oont-dry-sik
36	**sechsunddreißig**	zex-oont-dry-sik
37	**siebenunddreißig**	zeeben oont-dry-sik
38	**achtunddreißig**	*ah*kt-oont-dry-sik
39	**neununddreißig**	noyn-oont-dry-sik
40	**vierzig**	feer-tsik
41	**einundvierzig**	*i*ne-oont-feer-tsik
50	**fünfzig**	foonf-tsik
51	**einundfünfzig**	*i*ne-oont-foonf-tsik
60	**sechzig**	zek-tsik
61	**einundsechzig**	*i*ne-oont-zek-tsik
70	**siebzig**	zeep-tsik
71	**einundsiebzig**	*i*ne-oont-zeep-tsik
80	**achtzig**	*ah*k-tsik
81	**einundachtzig**	*i*ne-oont-ahk-tsik
90	**neunzig**	noyn-tsik
91	**einundneunzig**	*i*ne-oont-noyn-tsik
100	**hundert**	hoondert
101	**hunderteins**	hoondert-*i*nes
102	**hundertzwei**	hoondert-tsvy
125	**hundertfünfundzwanzig**	hoondert-f*oo*nf-oont-tsvan-tsik
150	**hundertfünfzig**	hoondert-f*oo*nf-tsik
175	**hundertfünfundsiebzig**	hoondert-f*oo*nf-oont-zeep-tsik
200	**zweihundert**	tsv*y*-hoondert
250	**zweihundertfünfzig**	tsv*y*-hoondert-f*oo*nf-tsik
300	**dreihundert**	dry-hoondert
400	**vierhundert**	feer-hoondert
500	**fünfhundert**	foonf-hoondert
700	**siebenhundert**	z*ee*ben-hoondert

1,000	**tausend**	towzent
1,100	**tausendeinhundert**	towzent-ine-hoondert
2,000	**zweitausend**	tsvy-towzent
5,000	**fünftausend**	foonf-towzent
10,000	**zehntausend**	tsain-towzent
100,000	**hunderttausend**	hoondert-towzent
1,000,000	**eine Million**	ineh mill-yon

Ordinal Numbers

1st	**erste**	airsteh
2nd	**zweite**	tsvy-teh
3rd	**dritte**	dritteh
4th	**vierte**	feerteh
5th	**fünfte**	foonfteh
6th	**sechste**	zexteh
7th	**siebte**	zeepteh
8th	**achte**	ahk-teh
9th	**neunte**	noynteh
10th	**zehnte**	tsainteh
11th	**elfte**	elfteh
12th	**zwölfte**	tsverlf-teh

Time

What time is it?	**Wie spät ist es?**
	vee shpait ist es
It's . . .	**Es ist ...**
	es ist
. . . one o'clock.	**ein Uhr.**
	ine oor
. . . two o'clock.	**zwei Uhr.**
	tsvy oor
. . . three o'clock.	**drei Uhr.**
	dry oor
. . . four o'clock.	**vier Uhr.**
	feer oor
. . . in the morning.	**morgens.**
	morgens
. . . in the afternoon.	**nachmittags.**
	nahk-mittahks
. . . in the evening.	**abends.**
	ah-bents

. . . at night.	**nachts.**
	nahkts
It's . . .	**Es ist ...**
	es ist
. . . noon.	**zwölf Uhr mittags.**
	tsverlf oor mittahks
. . . midnight.	**Mitternacht.**
	mitter-nakt
. . . five past five.	**fünf nach fünf.**
	foonf nahk foonf
. . . ten past five.	**zehn nach fünf.**
	tsain nahk foonf
. . . a quarter past five.	**viertel nach fünf.**
	feertel nahk foonf
. . . twenty past five.	**zwanzig nach fünf.**
	tsvahn-tsik nahk foonf
. . . twenty-five past five.	**fünf vor halb sechs.**
	foonf for hahlp zex
. . . half past five.	**halb sechs.**
	hahlp zex
. . . twenty-five to six.	**fünf nach halb sechs.**
	foonf nahk hahlp zex
. . . twenty to six.	**zwanzig vor sechs.**
	tsvahn-tsik for zex
. . . a quarter to six.	**viertel vor sechs.**
	feertel for zex
. . . ten to six.	**zehn vor sechs.**
	tsain for zex
. . . five to six.	**fünf vor sechs.**
	foonf for zex
At what time . . . (does the train leave)?	**Um wie viel Uhr ... (fährt der Zug ab)?**
	oom vee feel oor (fairt dair tsook up)
At . . .	**Um ...**
	oom
. . . 13.00.	**dreizehn Uhr.**
	dry-tsain oor
. . . 14.05.	**vierzehn Uhr fünf.**
	feer-tsain oor foonf
. . . 15.10.	**fünfzehn Uhr zehn.**
	foonf-tsain oor tsain
. . . 16.15.	**sechzehn Uhr fünfzehn.**
	zek-tsain oor foonf-tsain

. . . 17.20	**siebzehn Uhr zwanzig.**
	zeep-tsain oor tsvahn-tsik
. . . 18.25.	**achtzehn Uhr fünfundzwanzig.**
	ahk-tsain oor foonf-oont-
	tsvahn-tsik
. . . 19.30.	**neunzehn Uhr dreißig.**
	noyn-tsain oor dry-sik
. . . 20.35.	**zwanzig Uhr fünfunddreißig.**
	tsvahn-tsik oor foonf-oont-dry-sik
. . . 21.40.	**einundzwanzig Uhr vierzig.**
	ine-oon-tsvahn-tsik oor *feer*-tsik
. . . 22.45.	**zweiundzwanzig Uhr**
	fünfundvierzig.
	tsvy-oon-tsvahn-tsik oor foonf-
	oont-feer-tsik
. . . 23.50.	**dreiundzwanzig Uhr fünfzig.**
	dry-oon-tsvan-tsik oor foonf-tsik
. . . 0.55.	**null Uhr fünfundfünfzig.**
	nool oor foonf-oont-foonf-tsik
In ten minutes.	**In zehn Minuten.**
	in ts*ain* minooten
In a quarter of an hour.	**In einer Viertelstunde.**
	in *iner feertel-shtoondeh*
In half an hour.	**In einer halben Stunde.**
	in *iner hahlben shtoondeh*
In three-quarters of an hour.	**In einer Dreiviertelstunde.**
	in *iner dry-feertel-shtoondeh*

Days

Monday	**Montag**
	mone-tahk
Tuesday	**Dienstag**
	deens-tahk
Wednesday	**Mittwoch**
	mitt-voke
Thursday	**Donnerstag**
	donners-tahk
Friday	**Freitag**
	fry-tahk
Saturday	**Samstag/Sonnabend**
	zams-tahk/zonn-ahbent
Sunday	**Sonntag**
	zonn-tahk

last Monday	**letzten Montag** lets-ten mone-tahk
next Tuesday	**nächsten Dienstag** nexten deens-tahk
on Wednesday	**(am) Mittwoch** (um) mit-voke
on Thursdays	**donnerstags** doh-ners-tahks
until Friday	**bis Freitag** bis fry-tahk
before Saturday	**vor Samstag/Sonnabend** for zahms-tahk/zone-ahbent
after Sunday	**nach Sonntag** nahk zone-tahk
the day before yesterday	**vorgestern** for-ghestern
two days ago	**vor zwei Tagen** for tsvy tahg-en
yesterday	**gestern** ghestern
yesterday morning	**gestern morgen** ghestern morgen
yesterday afternoon	**gestern nachmittag** ghestern nahk-mittahk
last night	**gestern abend** ghestern ahbent
today	**heute** hoy-teh
this morning	**heute morgen** hoy-teh morgen
this afternoon	**heute nachmittag** hoy-teh nahk-mittahk
tonight	**heute abend** hoy-teh ahbent
tomorrow	**morgen** morgen
tomorrow morning	**morgen früh** morgen froo
tomorrow afternoon	**morgen nachmittag** morgen nahk-mittahk
tomorrow evening	**morgen abend** morgen ahbent
the day after tomorrow	**übermorgen** oober-morgen

Months, Seasons, and Dates

January	**Januar** *yah*-noo-ahr
February	**Februar** fay-broo-ahr
March	**März** mairts
April	**April** Ah-pril
May	**Mai** my
June	**Juni** *yoo*-nee
July	**Juli** *yoo*-lee
August	**August** ow-goost
September	**September** zeptember
October	**Oktober** oke-tober
November	**November** november
December	**Dezember** detsember
in January	**im Januar** im *yah*-noo-ahr
until February	**bis Februar** bis fay-broo-ahr
before March	**vor März** for mairts
after April	**nach April** nahk ah-pril
during May	**im Mai** im my
not until June	**nicht vor Juni** nisht for *yoo*-nee
the beginning of July	**Anfang Juli** anfang *yoo*-lee
the middle of August	**Mitte August** mitteh ow-goost
the end of September	**Ende September** endeh zeptember

last month	**(im) letzten Monat** (im) letsten monaht
this month	**diesen Monat** deezen monaht
next month	**nächsten Monat** nexten monaht
in spring	**im Frühling/Frühjahr** im frooling/froo-yar
in summer	**im Sommer** im zomer
in autumn	**im Herbst** im hairpst
in winter	**im Winter** im vinter
this year	**dieses Jahr** deezes yar
last year	**letztes Jahr** letstes yar
next year	**nächstes Jahr** nextes yar
in 1982	**im neunzehnhundertzweiundachtzig** noyn-tsain-hoondert-tsvy-oont-ahk-tsik
in 1985	**im neunzehnhundertfünfundachtzig** noyn-tsain-hoondert-foonf-oont-ahk-tsik
in 1990	**im neunzehnhundertneunzig** noyn-tsain-hoondert-noyn-tsik
What's the date today?	**Welches Datum haben wir heute?** velshes dah-toom hahben veer hoy-teh
It's the 6th of March.	**Heute ist der sechste März.** hoy-teh ist dair zexteh mairts
It's the 12th of April.	**Heute ist der zwölfte April.** hoy-teh ist dair tsverlf-teh ah-pril
It's the 21st of August.	**Heute ist der einundzwanzigste August.** hoy-teh ist dair ine-oont-tsvahnsix-teh ow-goost

Public Holidays

Unless otherwise specified, offices, shops, and schools are closed on the following days in Austria, Germany, and Switzerland.

1 January	**Neujahrstag**	New Year's Day
6 January	**Dreikönigsfest**	Epiphany (Austria only)
[*varies*]	**Karfreitag**	Good Friday (Germany and Switzerland)
[*varies*]	**Ostermontag**	Easter Monday
1 May	**Tag der Arbeit**	Labor Day (Austria and Germany)
[*varies*]	**Himmelfahrt**	Ascension
[*varies*]	**Pfingstmontag**	Whit Monday
[*varies*]	**Fronleichnam**	Corpus Christi (Austria and some regions of Germany)
15 August	**Mariä Himmelfahrt**	Assumption Day (Austria)
3 October	**Tag der Deutschen Einheit**	National Unity Day
26 October	**Nationalfeiertag**	National Day (Austria)
[*varies*]	**Buß- und Bettag**	Day of Prayer and Repentance (Germany)
8 December	**die Unbefleckte Empfängnis**	Immaculate Conception (Austria)
24 December	**Heiliger Abend**	Christmas Eve (half day)
25 December	**erster Weihnachtstag**	Christmas Day
26 December	**zweiter Weihnachtstag**	Boxing Day
26 December	**Stephanstag**	St. Stephen's Day (Austria and Switzerland)

Countries and Nationalities

Countries

Australia	**Australien**	owstrah-lee-en
Austria	**Österreich**	erster-rike
Belgium	**Belgien**	belg-ee-en
Britain	**Großbritannien**	gross-britahn-ee-en
Canada	**Kanada**	kah-nah-dah
Czech Republic	**die Tschechische Republik**	dee czechi-sheh repooblik

East Africa	**Ostafrika** oste-*ah*frikah
England	**England** eng-lunt
France	**Frankreich** fr*u*nk-rysh
Germany	**Deutschland** d*oy*tsh-lunt
Greece	**Griechenland** gr*ee*shen-lunt
Hungary	**Ungarn** *oo*n-garn
India	**Indien** *i*nd-ee-en
Ireland	**Irland** *ee*r-lunt
Italy	**Italien** it*ah*l-ee-en
Luxembourg	**Luxemburg** l*oo*xem-boork
Netherlands	**Holland** hollunt
New Zealand	**Neuseeland** noy-z*ay*-lunt
Northern Ireland	**Nordirland** nort-*ee*r-lunt
Pakistan	**Pakistan** p*ah*-kistahn
Poland	**Polen** p*oh*l-en
Portugal	**Portugal** port-oo-gahl
Russia	**Russland** r*oo*ss-lunt
Scotland	**Schottland** shot-lunt
South Africa	**Südafrika** zood-*ah*frikah
Spain	**Spanien** shp*ah*-nee-en
Switzerland	**die Schweiz** dee shvyts
to/for Switzerland	**in die Schweiz** in dee shvyts

in Switzerland	**in der Schweiz** in dair shvyts
United States	**die Vereinigten Staaten** dee fer-*ine*-nikten sht*ah*ten
to/for the United States	**in die Vereinigten Staaten** in dee fer-*ine*-nikten sht*ah*ten
in the United States	**in den Vereinigten Staaten** in den fer-*ine*-nikten sht*ah*ten
Wales	**Wales** wales
West Indies	**Westindien** vest-*ind*-ee-en

Nationalities

Where two alternatives are given, the first is used for males, the second for females.

American	**Amerikaner/Amerikanerin** ahmeri-*kah*-ner/ahmeri-*kah*-ner-in
Australian	**Australier/Australierin** owstr*ah*-lee-er/owstr*ah*-lee-er-in
British	**Brite/Britin** breeteh/breetin
Canadian	**Kanadier/Kanadierin** kah-*nah*-dee-er/kah-*nah*-dee-er-in
East African	**Ostafrikaner/Ostafrikanerin** oste-ahfrik*ah*-ner/ oste-ahfrik*ah*-ner-in
English	**Engländer/Engländerin** *eng*-lender/*eng*-lender-in
Indian	**Inder/Inderin** *in*der/*in*derin
Irish	**Ire/Irin** *ee*reh/*ee*rin
a New Zealander	**Neuseeländer/Neuseeländerin** noy-*zay*-lender/noy-*zay*-lender-in
a Pakistani	**Pakistaner/Pakistanerin** pahki-st*ah*n-er/pahki-st*ah*n-er-in
Scots	**Schotte/Schottin** sh*oh*tteh/sh*oh*ttin
South African	**Südafrikaner/Südafrikanerin** zood-afrik*ah*-ner/zood-afrik*ah*- ner-in

Welsh **Waliser/Waliserin**
vah-*lee*zer/vah-*lee*zer-in

West Indian **Westinder/Westinderin**
vest-*in*der/vest-*in*der-in

Department Store Guide

Alles für das Kind	Children's department
Auskunft	Information
Aussteuerartikel	Bridal shop
Babyausstattung	Layette
Babynahrung	Baby food
Bastelabteilung	Hobbies and crafts
Bettwäsche	Bedding, linen
Bilder und Rahmen	Paintings and frames
Blusen	Blouses
Brot	Bread
Bücher	Books
Büroartikel	Office supplies
Camping	Camping
Damenhüte	Millinery
Damenkonfektion/bekleidung	Ladies' wear
Damenwäsche	Lingerie
Delikatessen	Delicatessen
Dritte	Third
Elektrowaren	Electric appliances
Erdgeschoss	Ground floor
Erfrischungsraum	Refreshments
Erste	First
Etage	Floor
Fahrstühle	Elevators
Feinfrost	Frozen food
Fernsehen	Television
Frischfleisch	Fresh meat
Frisör	Hairdresser
Gardinen	Curtains
Geflügel	Poultry
Gemüse	Vegetables
Geschenkartikel	Gifts
Glas	Glassware
Haushaltswaren	Housewares

Heimwerker	Home improvement
Herrenartikel	Men's accessories
Herrenkonfektion/ bekleidung	Menswear
Kinderkonfektion/ bekleidung	Children's clothes
Kosmetikartikel	Cosmetics
Kücheneinrichtung	Kitchenware
Kurzwaren	Notions (sewing)
Lampen	Lamps
Lebensmittel	Food
Lederwaren	Leather goods
Miederwaren	Lingerie
Möbel	Furniture
Nähmaschinen	Sewing machines
Oberhemden	Shirts (department)
Obst	Fresh fruit
Parfümerie	Perfume section
Pelze	Furs
Photoartikel	Photography
Porzellan	China, porcelain
Putzmittel	Cleaning materials
Radio	Radio
Reisebüro	Travel agency
Rolltreppen	Escalators
Schallplatten	Records
Schmuck	Jewelry
Schnellimbiss	Snackbar
Schnittmuster	Sewing patterns
Schreibwaren	Stationery
Schuhe	Shoes
Spielwaren	Toys
Spirituosen	Spirits, liquors
Sportartikel	Sporting goods
Stock	Floor
Stoffe	Fabrics, drapery
Strickwaren	Knitwear
Strümpfe	Hosiery
Süßwaren	Sweets
Tabakwaren	Tobacco

Teppiche	Carpets
Tiefgeschoss	Basement
Toilettenartikel	Toiletries
Trikotagen	Knitwear
Umtauschkasse	Exchange and returns
Untergeschoss	Basement
Vierte	Fourth
Weine	Wine
Werkzeuge	Tools
Wolle	Wool
Wurstwaren	Sausages
Zeitungen	Newspapers
Zoo	Zoo
Zweite	Second

Conversion Tables

Metric/U.S. Systems

To convert from the metric to the U.S. system, read from the single digit in the center column to the number on the left; for example, 5 liters = 10.55 pints. To convert from the U.S. system to the metric, read from the single digit in the center column to the number on the right; for example, 5 pints = 2.35 liters.

PINTS		LITERS	GALLONS		LITERS
2.11	1	0.47	0.26	1	3.78
4.22	2	0.94	0.52	2	7.57
6.33	3	1.41	0.78	3	11.34
8.44	4	1.88	1.04	4	15.12
10.55	5	2.35	1.30	5	17.40
12.66	6	2.82	1.56	6	22.68
14.77	7	3.29	1.82	7	26.46
16.88	8	3.76	2.08	8	30.24
18.99	9	4.23	2.34	9	34.02
OUNCES		GRAMS	POUNDS		KILOS
0.04	1	28.35	2.20	1	0.45
0.07	2	56.70	4.41	2	0.91
0.11	3	85.05	6.61	3	1.36
0.14	4	113.40	8.82	4	1.81
0.18	5	141.75	11.02	5	2.27
0.21	6	170.10	13.23	6	2.72

0.25	7	198.45	15.43	7	3.18
0.28	8	226.80	17.64	8	3.63
0.32	9	255.15	19.84	9	4.08

INCHES		CENTIMETERS	YARDS		METERS
0.39	1	2.54	1.09	1	0.91
0.79	2	5.08	2.19	2	1.83
1.18	3	7.62	3.28	3	2.74
1.58	4	10.16	4.37	4	3.66
1.95	5	12.70	5.47	5	4.57
2.36	6	15.24	6.56	6	5.49
2.76	7	17.78	7.66	7	6.40
3.15	8	20.32	8.65	8	7.32
3.54	9	22.86	9.84	9	8.23

MILES		KILOMETERS
0.62	1	1.61
1.24	2	3.22
1.86	3	4.83
2.49	4	6.44
3.11	5	8.05
3.73	6	9.66
4.35	7	11.27
4.97	8	12.87
5.59	9	14.48

A quick way to convert kilometers to miles is to divide by 8 and multiply by 5. To convert miles to kilometers, divide by 5 and multiply by 8.

Temperature

FAHRENHEIT (F)	CELSIUS (C)	
212°	100°	boiling point of water
100°	38°	
98.4°	36.9°	body temperature
77°	25°	
68°	20°	
50°	10°	
32°	0°	freezing point of water
14°	−10°	
−4°	−20°	

To convert degrees Celsius to degrees Fahrenheit, divide by 5, multiply by 9, and add 32. To convert degrees Fahrenheit to degrees Celsius, subtract 32, divide by 9, and multiply by 5.

Tire Pressure

Pounds per Square Inch	Kilograms per Square Centimeter
22	1.5
29	2.0
35	2.5
43	3.0
45	3.2
50	3.5

Clothing Sizes

Always try on clothes before buying. Clothing sizes in conversion tables are often unreliable.

Women's Dresses and Suits

Europe	38	40	42	44	46	48
U.K.	32	34	36	38	40	42
U.S.	10	12	13	15	18	20

Men's Suits, Coats, and Jackets

Europe	46	48	50	52	54	56
U.K. and U.S.	36	38	40	42	44	46

Men's Shirts

Europe	36	37	38	39	41	42	43
U.K. and U.S.	14	14½	15	15½	16	16½	17

Socks

Europe	38–39	39–40	40–41	41–42	42–43
U.K. and U.S.	9½	10	10½	11	11½

Shoes

Europe	34	35½	36½	38	39	41	42	43	44	45
U.K.	2	3	4	5	6	7	8	9	10	11
U.S.	3½	4½	5½	6½	7½	8½	9½	10½	11½	12½

Do It Yourself: Some Notes on the German Language

This section does not deal with "grammar" as such. The purpose here is to explain some of the most obvious and elementary nuts and bolts of the language, based on the principal phrases included in the book. This information should enable you to produce numerous sentences of your own making.

Most of this section does not include help with pronunciation, partly because it would get in the way of the explanations and partly because you have to do it yourself at this stage if you are serious. Use the earlier examples in this book to figure out the German pronunciations in this section.

"The"

All nouns in German belong to one of three genders: masculine, feminine, or neuter, regardless of whether they refer to living things or inanimate objects.

"THE" SINGULAR

	MASCULINE	FEMININE	NEUTER
the address		die Adresse	
the apple	der Apfel		
the bill		die Rechnung	
the cup of tea		die Tasse Tee	
the glass of beer			das Glas Bier
the ham sandwich			das Schinkenbrot
the key	der Schlüssel		
the luggage			das Gepäck
the menu		die Speisekarte	
the newspaper		die Zeitung	
the receipt		die Quittung	
the suitcase	der Koffer		
the telephone directory			das Telefonbuch
the timetable	der Fahrplan		

"THE" PLURAL

the addresses	**die Adressen**
the apples	**die Äpfel**
the bills	**die Rechnungen**
the cups of tea	**die Tassen Tee**
the glasses of beer	**die Gläser Bier**
the ham sandwiches	**die Schinkenbrote**
the keys	**die Schlüssel**
the menus	**die Speisekarten**
the newspapers	**die Zeitungen**
the receipts	**die Quittungen**
the suitcases	**die Koffer**
the telephone directories	**die Telefonbücher**
the timetables	**die Fahrpläne**

Important Things to Remember

- It is difficult to predict whether a noun is masculine, feminine, or neuter. So learn the gender of each noun as you learn the noun itself. Nouns ending in **-ung**, **-keit**, and **-heit** are feminine and nouns ending in **-chen** and **-lein** are neuter, but this rule accounts for relatively few words.

- In the tables, *the* is **der** before masculine nouns, **die** before feminine nouns, **das** before neuter nouns. Does it matter? Not unless you want to make a serious attempt to speak correctly and scratch beneath the surface of the language. You would be understood if you said **das Speisekarte** or **die Fahrplan**, provided your pronunciation was good.

- In the word list *the* is **die** before any plural noun (not to be confused with the feminine **die**).

- There is no easy way to remember how to spell German nouns in the plural. (It may help to think of the plurals of *ox*, *goose*, and *sheep* in English. All three plurals are formed differently.) The following are five ways that German nouns are made plural:

  Add **-en**, **-n**, or **-nen**.
  Change a vowel sound by adding an umlaut **ä**, **ö**, or **ü**.
  Add **-er**, usually with an umlaut on an **a**, **o**, or **u**.
  Add **-e**, often with an umlaut on an **a**, **o**, or **u**.
  Add **-s** to an imported foreign word such as **Hotel**.

The methods are easy enough, but knowing which method to apply to which noun is a different matter. In this section, the spelling of nouns in the plural form are given for you: try to learn them by heart as you practice them.

Practice saying and writing these sentences in German:

Where is the key?	**Wo ist der Schlüssel?**
Where is the receipt?	**Wo ist ... ?**
Where is the address?	
Where is the luggage?	
Where are the keys?	**Wo sind die Schlüssel?**
Where are the ham sandwiches?	**Wo sind ... ?**
Where are the newspapers?	
Where are the apples?	

Now make up more similar sentences. Try adding *please* (**bitte**) at the beginning or end.

! Caution

In phrases beginning with

> Do you have the . . . ?
> I'd like the . . . .
> Where can I get the . . . ?

the masculine singular nouns (e.g., *apple, key, suitcase, timetable*) are tricky. Quite simply, the word *der* (*the*) has to change to **den**. This situation is usually called the accusative case, but it affects only the masculine singular.

Der Apfel becomes **den Apfel**.
Der Schlüssel becomes **den Schlüssel**.
Der Koffer becomes **den Koffer**.
Der Fahrplan becomes **den Fahrplan**.

In this section, a caution sign indicates a masculine noun in the accusative case.

Practice saying and writing these sentences in German. (Note the caution signs.)

! Do you have the key?	**Haben Sie den Schlüssel?**
! Do you have the suitcase?	**Haben Sie ... ?**
Do you have the luggage?	
Do you have the telephone directory?	
Do you have the menu?	
! I'd like the key.	**Ich möchte ... Schlüssel.**

! I'd like the timetable.
I'd like the bill.
I'd like the receipt.
I'd like the keys.
! Where can I get the key?   **Wo kann man ... Schlüssel bekommen?**

Where can I get the address?
Where can I get the timetables?

Now make up more similar sentences. Try adding *please* (**bitte**) at the beginning or end.

"A"/"An" and "Some"/"Any"

"A"/"AN"

	MASCULINE	FEMININE	NEUTER
an address		**eine Adresse**	
an apple	**ein Apfel**		
a bill		**eine Rechnung**	
a cup of tea		**eine Tasse Tee**	
a glass of beer			**ein Glas Bier**
a ham sandwich			**ein Schinkenbrot**
a key	**ein Schlüssel**		
a menu		**eine Speisekarte**	
a newspaper		**eine Zeitung**	
a receipt		**eine Quittung**	
a suitcase	**ein Koffer**		
a telephone directory			**ein Telefonbuch**
a timetable	**ein Fahrplan**		

"SOME"/"ANY" (PLURAL)

addresses	**Adressen**
apples	**Äpfel**
receipts	**Rechnungen**
cups of tea	**Tassen Tee**
glasses of beer	**Gläser Bier**
ham sandwiches	**Schinkenbrote**
keys	**Schlüssel**
menus	**Speisekarten**
newspapers	**Zeitungen**
receipts	**Quittungen**

suitcases	**Koffer**
telephone directories	**Telefonbücher**
timetables	**Fahrpläne**

Important Things to Remember

* In the tables, *a* or *an* is **ein** before a masculine noun, **eine** before a feminine noun, and **ein** before a neuter noun.

* *Some* or *any* before a noun in the plural has no equivalent in German; so leave it out.

! Caution

In phrases beginning with

> Do you have . . . ?
> I'd like . . .
> Where can I get . . . ?
> Is there . . . ?
> Are there . . . ?
> I'll have . . .
> I need . . .

the masculine singular nouns are tricky. Quite simply, the word **ein** (*a/an*) has to change to **einen**. In these examples of the accusative case, only the masculine singular nouns are affected.

Ein Apfel becomes **einen Apfel**.
Ein Schlüssel becomes **einen Schlüssel**.
Ein Koffer becomes **einen Koffer**.
Ein Fahrplan becomes **einen Fahrplan**.

Practice saying and writing these sentences in German. (Note the caution signs.)

Do you have a receipt?	**Haben Sie eine ... ?**
! Do you have an apple?	
I'd like a telephone directory.	**Ich möchte ein ...**
! I'd like a timetable.	
I'd like (some) ham sandwiches.	
Where can I get a cup of tea?	**Wo kann man eine ... bekommen?**
! Where can I get a suitcase?	
Where can I get (some) newspapers?	
Is there a menu?	**Gibt es hier eine ... ?**
! Is there a key?	**Gibt es hier ... ?**
! Is there a timetable?	

Are there (any) keys?	**Gibt es hier ... ?**
Are there (any) newspapers?	
Are there (any) ham sandwiches?	
I'll have a glass of beer.	**Ich hätte gern ein ...**
I'll have a cup of tea.	**Ich hätte gern ...**
! I'll have an apple.	
I'll have (some) apples.	
I'll have (some) ham sandwiches.	
I need a receipt.	**Ich brauche eine ...**
! I need a suitcase.	
I need a cup of tea.	
! I need a key.	
I need (some) addresses.	
I need (some) ham sandwiches.	

Now make up more similar sentences.

"Some"/"Any"

In cases where *some* or *any* refer to more than one thing, such as *some/any newspapers* and *some/any tomatoes*, there is no German equivalent, as explained earlier.

some/any newspapers	**Zeitungen**
some/any tomatoes	**Tomaten**

As a guide, when *some/any* is meant, you can usually count the number of containers or whole items.

In cases where *some* refers to part of a whole thing or an indefinite quantity, the word **etwas** can be used. Neither the gender of the noun nor the accusative case pose problems. Look at the following list and complete it.

the butter	**die Butter**	**etwas Butter**	some butter
the bread	**das Brot**	**etwas Brot**	some bread
the cheese	**der Käse**	**etwas Käse**	some cheese
the coffee	**der Kaffee**	**etwas Kaffee**	some coffee
the ice cream	**das Eis**	...	some ice cream
the lemonade	**die Limonade**	...	some lemonade
the pineapple	**die Ananas**	...	some pineapple
the sugar	**der Zucker**	...	some sugar
the tea	**der Tee**	...	some tea
the water	**das Wasser**	...	some water
the wine	**der Wein**	...	some wine

Etwas is not essential, however, and can just be left out altogether.

Practice saying and writing these sentences in German.

Do you have some coffee?	**Haben Sie etwas Kaffee?**
	Haben Sie Kaffee?

Do you have some ice cream?
Do you have some lemonade?
Do you have some pineapple?
I'd like some butter.
I'd like some sugar.
I'd like some bread.
Where can I get some cheese?
Where can I get some ice cream?
Where can I get some water?
Is there any lemonade?
Is there any water?
Is there any wine?
I'll have some butter.
I'll have some tea.
I'll have some coffee.
I need some sugar.
I need some butter.
I need some coffee.

"This" and "That"

Dies (*this*) and **das** (*that*) are two helpful words in German. If you don't know the German name for an object, just point and say one of the following phrases.

Ich möchte das.	I'd like that.
Ich hätte gern dies.	I'll have this.
Ich brauche das.	I need that.

Helping Others

You can help yourself by using phrases modeled after the following.

I'd like . . . a ham sandwich.	**Ich möchte ... ein Schinkenbrot.**
Where can I get . . . a cup of tea?	**Wo kann man ... eine Tasse Tee bekommen?**
I'll have . . . a glass of beer.	**Ich hätte gern ... ein Glas Bier.**
I need . . . a receipt.	**Ich brauche ... eine Quittung.**

If you meet another English speaker having trouble making him- or herself understood, you should be able to speak German on that person's behalf.

He'd like . . .	**Er möchte ein Schinkenbrot.** er mershteh ine shinken-brote
She'd like . . .	**Sie möchte ein Schinkenbrot.** zee mershteh ine shinken-brote

Strictly speaking, **Kann man ... ?** means "Can one . . . ?" and normally serves instead of "Can I . . . ?" (**Kann ich ... ?**), "Can he . . . ?", "Can she . . . ?", "Can they . . . ?", and "Can we . . . ?" However, all of the just-mentioned variations in German are included in the remainder of this section because of their potential usefulness.

Where can he get . . . ?	**Wo kann er eine Tasse Tee bekommen?** vo kahnn er ineh tahsseh tay ba-komen
Where can she get . . . ?	**Wo kann sie eine Tasse Tee bekommen?** vo kahn zee ineh tahsseh tay ba-kohmen
He'll have . . .	**Er hätte gern ein Glas Bier.** air hetteh gairn ine glahs beer
She'll have . . .	**Sie hätte gern ein Glas Bier.** zee hetteh gairn ine glahs beer
He needs . . .	**Er braucht eine Quittung.** er bra-ookt ineh kvittoong
She needs . . .	**Sie braucht eine Quittung.** zee bra-ookt ineh kvittoong

You can also help a couple or a group if *they* are having difficulties. The German word for *they* is the same as the word for *she* and *you*: **sie**. But there is a difference, which is fairly easy to detect.

They'd like . . .	**Sie möchten (etwas) Käse.** zee mershten (etvahs) kay-zeh
Where can they get . . . ?	**Wo können sie (etwas) Butter bekommen?** vo kernen zee (etvahs) booter ba-komen
They'll have . . .	**Sie hätten gern (etwas) Wein.** zee hetten gairn (etvahs) vine
They need . . .	**Sie brauchen (etwas) Wasser.** zee bra-ooken (etvahs) vahsser

What about the two of you? No problem. The word for *we* is **wir**.

We'd like . . .	**Wir möchten (etwas) Wein.**
	veer m*e*rshten (*etvahs*) vine
Where can we get . . .?	**Wo können wir (etwas) Wasser**
	bekommen?
	vo k*e*rnen veer (*etvahs*) v*ah*sser
	ba-komen
We'll have . . .	**Wir hätten gern (etwas) Butter.**
	veer hetten g*ai*rn (*etvahs*) booter
We need . . .	**Wir brauchen (etwas) Zucker.**
	veer br*a*-oo*k*en (*etvahs*) tsoocker

More Practice

Here are some more German names for things. Using the information in this section, see how many different sentences you can make up.

	SINGULAR	PLURAL
ashtray	**Aschenbecher (m)**	**Aschenbecher**
bag	**Tasche (f)**	**Taschen**
ball-point pen	**Kugelschreiber (m)**	**Kugelschreiber**
bottle	**Flasche (f)**	**Flaschen**
car	**Auto (n)**	**Autos**
cigarette	**Zigarette (f)**	**Zigaretten**
corkscrew	**Korkenzieher (m)**	**Korkenzieher**
egg	**Ei (n)**	**Eier**
house	**Haus (n)**	**Häuser**
knife	**Messer (n)**	**Messer**
mountain	**Berg (m)**	**Berge**
plate	**Teller (m)**	**Teller**
postcard	**Postkarte (f)**	**Postkarten**
room	**Zimmer (n)**	**Zimmer**
shoe	**Schuh (m)**	**Schuhe**
stamp	**Briefmarke (f)**	**Briefmarken**
street	**Straße (f)**	**Straßen**
ticket	**Fahrkarte (f)**	**Fahrkarten**
train	**Zug (m)**	**Züge**
wallet	**Brieftasche (f)**	**Brieftaschen**

Index